EXCITING ICT IN
HISTORY

Ben Walsh

Published by Network Educational Press Ltd
PO Box 635
Stafford
ST16 1BF

First published 2005
© Ben Walsh 2005

ISBN 185539 190 2

Managing Editor: Sarah Nunn
Cover design: Neil Hawkins, NEP
Layout: Neil Hawkins, NEP
Illustrations: Katherine Baxter

Printed in Great Britain by MPG Books Ltd, Bodmin, Cornwall

Contents

Foreword

I have had the great honour and pleasure to travel a lot of the world for over a decade talking, advising and consulting about ICT and learning. It is a personal passion and, being married to a teacher, an issue that concerns me both professionally and personally. When I started I met many enthusiasts who shared a dream that we could use ICT to transform the experience of education and deliver a global aspiration of education for every citizen of the world. Against these lofty ambitions the perennial constraints of budgets, political will and professional inertia were easily visible. There were many fears expressed to me. Most importantly, there was a concern that, somehow, ICT would be used as an excuse to sack teachers and close schools and pump learning into kids' heads through impersonal technology.

Being an optimist, my experience over the last decade has kept those lofty aspirations alive. It has also made the fundamental truths about both education and learning clear to me. First, learning is at its heart a social and a socializing experience. ICTs are very powerful tools, but smart technologies need smart people, they don't replace them. In a world where technology is increasingly pervasive, teachers become more not less important.

Second, as the world becomes increasingly connected, as technology and science develop at an ever increasing pace, the economic and social future of any country is increasingly tied to its commitment to education and training, not just for the elite but for every citizen and community.

Third, the goal is not just raising standards but changing culture. I describe this using the analogy of the driving test, a rite of passage for many young people. The emerging global information society requires us to create a new generation who, when they leave school, put on their L-plates and think 'I am a learner', rather than take them off and say 'I have passed'.

We can only make this happen on the scale needed if we value and invest in our teachers as lifelong learners themselves, not just in their 'subject skills'. To do this we need to marry the Big Picture of a transformed experience of learning to ICT practice, but also to new theories of learning such as learning styles or multiple intelligences. For teachers to be seen as learners themselves we need to build bridges between different areas of research – in education, learning theories, ICT and management, to name but a few.

Reading the first few titles in this series, it is wonderful to see words like creativity, personalization and exciting being based on actual evidence, not just lofty aspiration. The rate of change of technology in the next decade will at least match the progress in the last. The materials available to enrich good teaching and learning practice will grow exponentially. None of this will have the profound change that many aspire to if we cannot build the bridge between theory and what happens in individual lessons, be they in art, maths, music, history, modern languages or any other area of the curriculum.

The notion of ICT as a tool across the curriculum was greeted sceptically a decade ago. Many professionals told me that ICT may be important in maths or science, but irrelevant in the arts and humanities. My own experience is that the most exciting innovations have actually been in arts and humanities, while the notion of maths as a visual discipline seemed alien a few years ago. It has not been ICT but innovative teachers, researchers and indeed publishers who have pushed the art of the possible.

In a lot of my work, I have encouraged the notion that we should see the era we live in as a New Renaissance, rather than a new Industrial Revolution. While the industrial revolutions were about simplification and analysis, the era we live in is about synthesis and connection. We need our learners to embrace both depth and breadth to meet their needs to learn for life and living.

To the authors of this series, I offer my congratulations and sincere thanks. In bringing together the evidence of what works, the digital resources available and the new theories of learning, along with the new capabilities of ICT, they bring the focus onto the most important element of the transformation of learning, which to me is the learning needs of the teaching profession.

To the readers of this series, I make what I believe is my boldest claim. This is the greatest time in human history to be a teacher. Our societies and economies demand education like never before. Our increasing knowledge of how we learn and how the brain works, together with the availability of powerful ICT tools, make this a time when the creativity, professionalism and aspirations for a learning society are at a premium. Teaching is a noble profession. It is after all the profession that creates all the others.

There are many things that we do not yet know, so much to learn. That is what makes this so exciting. I and my colleagues at Microsoft can build the tools, but we believe that it is putting those tools in the hands of innovative, skilled and inspirational teachers that creates the real value.

I hope that after reading any of the books in this series you will feel the excitement that will make learning come alive both for you and the children you teach.

Best wishes.

Chris Yapp
Head of Public Sector Innovation
Microsoft Ltd

Author's acknowledgements

I would like to express my gratitude to Lez Smart of Goldsmiths College for his guidance and ideas on the use of ICT in primary school history. Rick Weights, deputy headteacher at Athelstan community primary school in North Yorkshire, also provided invaluable feedback on ICT in primary school history. I would also like to acknowledge my debt to many members of HABET, the Historical Association Advisory Body on Educational Technology. It has taken a while but the hard work of these pioneers is now making a genuine impact in many classrooms. Many others have also blazed their own particular trails ranging from the early simulation programs to the latest websites. Finally, let me thank the many teachers who have tried out materials and ideas and reported back their triumphs and disasters and particularly their (and my) long-suffering students who have put up with years of acting as guinea pigs for new ideas involving technology.

Preface

The aim of this resource is very simple. It is to explore a wide range of different ways in which the use of ICT can enhance the teaching and learning of history in the primary and secondary school classroom. There are two elements to the resource – the book and the accompanying CD-ROM. The book itself is a resource which is designed to stand alone. It is not necessary to sit down next to a computer as you look through each chapter! On the other hand, in many instances this would be an extremely effective way to get the full impact of what is being put forward.

The package of book and CD-ROM is very much aimed at a range of teachers. It is not a technical self-help tutorial course, and offers little if any specific instruction on particular pieces of software or technical operations. Neither is this package a collection of teaching resources, although many of the websites and exemplar material to be found on the CD-ROM can be used (and have been used) in the classroom. There are many references to such resources in the text and to make it easier these resources are highlighted in the margins with the words 'CD-ROM' or 'WEBSITE'. The word 'CD-ROM' indicates that the resource being referred to in the text is actually located on the CD-ROM. This will usually be a word processor, data handling or presentation file. The word 'WEBSITE' indicates that there is a shortcut on the CD-ROM to the website being referred to. This combination of book and CD-ROM is therefore very much a resource designed to develop thinking and practice in the pedagogy of using ICT in the history classroom. That said, it also tries to give teachers a sense of the wider issues and perspectives that inevitably assume some importance when the use of ICT is involved.

The materials on the CD-ROM are organized using the same structure as the book. If you are reading chapter 3 and want to look at the resource used in figure 3.1a for example, then simply open the CD-ROM and select chapter 3. The file name of the resource in figure 3.1a is Vikings, so simply open this file. In some chapters there are a large number of files. In these chapters, many files are grouped into sub folders (such as *archive* collections in chapter 5). The margin feature in the book indicating a CD-ROM resource also indicates whether the file is in a sub folder.

CD-ROM Ch3/Vikings

CD-ROM Ch4/Huntington Jail–
          Prisoner Activities Word doc

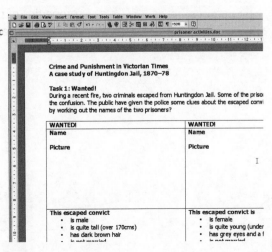

Chapters 1 and 2 focus very much on the wider perspective. Chapter 1 is a plea to put ICT in its place. This phrase made much more sense in the mid 1990s when ICT was known as IT. 'Putting IT in its place' was the headline for a pamphlet produced by the History and IT Support Project. This was a joint venture between the Historical Association and National Council for Educational Technology (NCET) or BECTA (British Education Communications and Technology Agency) as it is now known. The spirit of 'Putting IT in its place' is at the heart of this book and, I am delighted to see, is now at the heart of government thinking about ICT in the curriculum. Increasingly, the focus is on embedding ICT in curriculum subjects. Chapter 2 is very much about how this might be done. It looks at the potential problems and pitfalls but also at the possibilities. Above all, it focuses on the pedagogy and planning needed to make the use of ICT an enjoyable and meaningful experience for students and teachers. This is just as important as any technical knowledge or expertise. The role of the CD-ROM in these chapters is to provide easy access to the websites mentioned in each chapter, acting as a portal to the organizations and resources described. The CD-ROM also provides some exemplar materials from Nelson Thornes' *Empires and Citizens* series and Hodder Murray's *GCSE Modern World History e-learning edition*. *Exciting ICT in History* is designed to stand alone as a resource to support teachers. However, the book and accompanying CD-ROM probably work most effectively when used together so that the resources and pedagogical insights raised in the book can be illustrated clearly and explored thoroughly in a hands-on situation.

Every teacher who uses ICT has his or her pet projects, favourite resources and number one software package. Chapters 3–7 are designed to explore a wide range of software applications and what they might add to the teaching and learning process in history. All of these chapters look at how ICT applications can help with issues that arise from the teaching of history. Thus, in chapter 3 the focus is on how the word processor helps us to help students grapple with thorny issues such as historical interpretations and analytical writing. Similarly, the chapters on data handling, the internet, authoring and digital video all examine the ways in which these resources help us to help students develop their thinking. The corresponding chapters of the CD-ROM contain web links and/or appropriate resources for all of the activities featured in the book. In some cases the resources are gathered by themes such as Ancient Egypt, the Irish Famine and so on. This will make them easier to locate when looking for resources referred to in the corresponding book chapter. All of the resources can be used in the classroom with students but it should be remembered that their primary purpose is to illustrate the properties of particular software or resources for particular purposes in history teaching. I hope that they can be used to good effect for both.

Chapter 1

A forward vision

In this section you will discover:

- ICT offers the opportunities and the resources for learners in history lessons to have fantastic media rich experiences – ideal at a time when teachers are becoming increasingly aware that students have a range of learning styles and that different types of information input are more effective for different learners.

- ICT allows students to access and achieve wondrous possibilities, from picking the brains of an academic expert on another continent to creating multimedia products – a new dimension for students to demonstrate their understanding.

- There is a real danger of disillusionment on the part of teachers and learners who experience a gap between the rhetoric of what ICT can do for learning and the reality of what can really be achieved with ICT.

- Effective learning is determined by the quality of teacher planning. ICT resources need to fit in with this planning, not the other way around.

- ICT can enhance teaching and learning in history, and this need not involve complex or expensive hardware or software.

- We are still at an early stage in terms of getting the most from ICT. Video recorders/players are now a staple resource in the history classroom, but it took many years to maximize their potential use.

I have often sat in a conference hall full of enthusiastic and excited educationalists, listening to some ICT guru (usually a man) outline his vision of learning in the future. Strangely, these gurus rarely choose history as their example for this future vision, so let me have a go.

Selling Dunkirk in 1940:
A multimedia investigation in the near future

Picture a young learner in the early years of secondary school a few years from now. On a typical day, he arrives at school and looks up his individual learning programme, carefully negotiated with his personal tutor. ICT provides access to all the resources our young friend can ever need, so his school has decided that lessons with 30 students or so are out of date. Students have learning programmes and their teachers are now more like consultants.

The programme shows that our student needs to work on his history assignment. He heads off to his learning space where he plugs in his personal identity code and logs onto his ongoing assignment. It's progressing but there is still some work to do. His assignment is to examine how people in Britain reacted to the Dunkirk evacuation in May 1940. Did they really rally around the government or was this simply an illusion created by the government information machine?

The first section of his assignment has gone well. He has looked at the scale of the military disaster that was Dunkirk and presented lots of data on casualties, loss of equipment – convincing proof that militarily Dunkirk was a defeat. He has also analysed the way the media and the government came together to present (some might say 'spin') the Dunkirk evacuation. He was helped by the fact that the BBC's media correspondent put an article on the BBC News website on the anniversary of Dunkirk looking at this very issue. However, his teacher, as always, wants just that little bit more out of him. She can view his developing assignment courtesy of a content management system that allows her to look at our young friend's published work area. She has sent an email asking him to try and find some original source material that demonstrates that at least some people were a bit cynical about the media coverage of Dunkirk.

Our young learner manages to do this from another BBC resource, called People's War. A search on Dunkirk has located many comments on the events of 1940 and our learner has selected the most appropriate – some of which are audio recordings. He then thinks he might find some more interesting material if he goes to the Imperial War Museum website where more recordings can be found. Finally, he starts looking for evidence that government media plans worked or failed. Where better to look for this than the website of the National Archives. Here he finds a selection of official documents setting out government instructions to newspapers and the BBC on how to report on Dunkirk. He also finds some 'rushes' (unedited news film) of Dunkirk from the British Pathe website which show how the coverage was carefully selected and the required level of spin was achieved.

Fig 1.1

ICT resources create the opportunity for all students to answer important historical questions such as these.

There's only one thing missing now – some academic gravitas to give weight to his thesis. He decides to contact a leading university academic for his views on Dunkirk and the media via a video conferencing link. The academic is unavailable; however, he gets a lot of queries like this and has placed a number of short monologues of his views on his web page. Our learner selects an appropriate 30 second piece from a larger monologue entitled 'The Dunkirk Spirit'.

Now our learner has everything he needs. He takes his raw material and puts it together using a video editing package. He sends an email to his teacher saying that his work is finished. She is then able to go into his published work area and view a short documentary which:

➡ analyses the events at Dunkirk

➡ considers (in a voice-over scripted and recorded by our learner) the evidence that the government and media worked together to present Dunkirk in a particular way

➡ shows examples of the evidence in the form of media clips (with a text commentary written by our learner running beneath the clips) and extracts from newspapers (which are recorded by our learner and played back as an audio track)

➡ explores the possibility that not everybody swallowed the story by using 'talking head' extracts of the academic historian and the contemporaries whose testimonies were examined on the BBC website.

▌ Rhetoric and reality

Our future vision is an intriguing and inviting picture, is it not? It certainly presses all the right educational 'buttons':

➡ Learning styles: Working in this autonomous fashion should allow our student to work and demonstrate his understanding in his preferred learning style. He could focus his research on particular types of sources (text, audio, still or moving image). He can work at his own particular learning pace.

➡ A real task: There is little doubt that the assignment presented our student with a genuine challenge. Challenge is a key issue in all areas of education, not least because challenge is so closely linked with the expectations we have of students which in turn affect their performance. It is no coincidence that programmes such as the Critical Skills Programme, being pioneered in many UK schools, put student challenges at the heart of the learning processes they advocate.

➡ Community: The focus on an event such as Dunkirk would fit perfectly with the ethos of schools which are looking to build closer links between the learning in schools and the experiences of real people, potentially even individuals in their local communities. Dunkirk affected virtually everyone in Britain in some way, so this task contains the potential to bring our student into contact with local people who remember or even experienced the event. This would fit well with our current concerns that history, and education generally, is becoming increasingly faced with a 'So what?' response.

Just as exciting, the scenario here is achievable today with readily available technology:

➡ BBC News, History and People's War websites are already up and running

➡ A vast array of original newsreel clips is already available free, online from British Pathe – more archives seem likely to open up their collections in the near future

➡ The National Archives is arguably the UK's premier educational website for history, certainly for primary sources

➡ The Imperial War Museum has a growing web presence

➡ Video conferencing and 'talking head' video files are well-established technologies

➡ The ability to record audio onto a computer has been around for a long time

➡ Video editing packages are now readily available. A laptop computer can now handle operations which only ten years ago would have required roomfuls of equipment.

It would be understandable to ask at this juncture – if all these wondrous things are possible, then why aren't they happening? – but it would also be missing the point. It would be a case of falling for the rhetoric of the more extreme ICT enthusiasts instead of considering the realities of *how* learners learn. As teachers, we are regularly bombarded with utopian claims about the transformative power of ICT, but are these claims borne out in the practice and experience of most of us who have tried to use ICT in the teaching of history?

Let us leave aside the most obvious constraint on the use of ICT, which is that in most primary and secondary schools there are simply not enough computers. That is why my hypothetical example was set some years from now – the rather optimistic assumption being that this problem has been solved! Let's concentrate on our learner in this example. There is no doubt that existing available technology means that he could access those BBC websites, the National Archives and the online academic. He could take all of those media resources and knit them into an impressive documentary.

On the other hand, why would he in the environment set out in our example? Technology enthusiasts point to a future where learning is individualized. They talk of students being responsible for their own learning. This often translates into a vision in which schools, classrooms, teachers and classes are effectively marginalized. In this scenario, our learner *could* access the resources listed, but it would be a remarkable feat of planning and intuition if he were to bother to do so. The caption to figure 1.1 on page 10 points out that ICT would enable our learner to *answer* all of these questions, but it is hard to see how ICT, as opposed to a teacher, would get our young friend to *ask* these questions in the first place. Which of the two is more important?

In our hypothetical example, our learner follows a complex path of enquiry and decision making. Without teacher guidance, he might get lucky and find the BBC website on the media management of Dunkirk. He just might squeeze the maximum value from the article without a teacher's guidance and support, but we are now beginning to stretch credibility a little.

In the next stage of the assignment, our learner then plans to trawl through a different segment of the BBC's resources (not always the most joined up of sites). He then searches the resources of the National Archives and the Imperial War Museum, showing a 'bloodhound like' ability to use search engines and to sift through information that is relevant or irrelevant to his enquiry.

We are now stretching credibility quite a lot, and it's getting more stretched all the time. Without guidance, how likely would it be for our learner to independently have thought of going to a particular academic's web page for an interview? How realistic is it for our learner to think of creating a documentary, learn the relevant editing skills and absorb sufficient of the techniques and processes used by film makers without a high level of instruction and input, to say nothing of reflection and discussion with peers and teachers? In short, the fact that these technologies and resources exist in no way guarantees that learners will use them efficiently, effectively, creatively – or at all! This is not meant to sound negative, purely realistic – even optimistic. It is simply an argument not to get carried away with false expectations of what technology can achieve. ICT can transform activities in such a way that they enable a range of approaches so that the different learning styles of students are addressed.

History and ICT: Developing a vision

These questions are at the heart of what this book is all about. ICT is a resource, a tool for investigating and communicating and a subject discipline that develops critical thinking and presentational skills. Together, history and ICT can achieve much more than they can separately.

From the teacher's point of view, whether you are a secondary specialist or a primary teacher trying to combine history with literacy or indeed ICT, this book is about what you might want to do in your classroom, and the ways in which ICT might help you achieve them. It also provides suggestions as to how ICT offers opportunities to enhance learning in history by:

➡ working in different ways, such as using word-processing to help students to read a contemporary text for its hidden meanings

➡ accessing resources previously not available at all, such as records from a local or overseas archive

➡ using aspects of ICT functionality, such as the ability of data handling software to group and sort large datasets to find patterns of migration, employment and so on

➡ exploiting the use of ICT to demonstrate links with current political situations, or links with citizenship or the vocational dimension of the curriculum.

This book examines the ways in which we as history teachers might be able to bridge the gap between rhetoric and reality. Unless our learner is an abnormally gifted individual, he needs to be taught, as well as to learn. Most learners develop, at least in part, as a result of socially constructed learning. In other words, students learn by interacting with other students and with the teacher. These interactions introduce new perspectives, new approaches and new information. The interactions between student and teacher also help to model ways of thinking and working for students. In short, students learn to work better by watching the teacher work. The problem-solving skills our student shows in our hypothetical example are not unattainable by any means. Many a primary school student will display several of them in the course of any enquiry. Plenty of students at KS3 will also develop these skills. The key point is, however, that ICT merely affords the opportunity to use them. The problem-solving skills and thought processes themselves will be developed in the course of carefully planned enquiries which take students through historical content, historical processes and make students aware of the processes they are carrying out.

We as teachers will eventually, we hope, help students to develop into the kind of learner described in our example, but the kind of initiative shown in the example takes time for most young people to develop, and they will not develop these abilities without communicating – with their peers and with their teachers. The value of such collaborative approaches is spelled out by Colin Weatherley (2003):

Many people have observed that, while CSP [Critical Skills Programme] challenges are a powerful way of enabling pupils to develop subject knowledge and understanding, the emphasis on developing such a collaborative learning community is an equally powerful way of promoting pupils' personal and social development.

Bridging the reality gap: Some inspirational examples

Looking at all of these lofty aims and potential hazards can be a trifle daunting. The best way to overcome this trepidation is to look at a few examples of good practice. They range widely in terms of scale, ambition and setting. However, all have at their core a clear plan about how ICT can enhance learning, whether that be in history or in ICT.

Example 1: Website of Snaith Primary School

WEBSITE   http://home.freeuk.net/elloughton13/index.htm

This wonderful site is an example of a website developed by teachers for their students. What's more, it actually says so! There are so many gems to be unearthed in this site, such as the Viking village of Snayfwickby.

Perhaps even more impressive is the creative writing resource based on the Aztecs (figure 1.2). Here students are given easily digested information and some prompts to create their own stories. It's an excellent example of where history, literacy and ICT all meet in a cross-curricular feast, which is fully in line with the aims of the Primary National Strategy (http://www.standards.dfes.gov.uk/primary).

WEBSITE

The history provides the context for the work, in this instance the Aztecs. The historical activities are valid and stimulating. Students demonstrate their understanding of different features of a past non-European society by looking at such areas as religious belief, daily commercial life, science, culture, architecture. The mechanism for demonstrating this understanding is creative writing. This provides a stimulating vehicle for literacy work with the potential to write in different genres.

The use of ICT makes an important contribution in several different ways. The use of the website allows students to choose between eight different topics as the subject of their written work. The use of a website makes this element of choice considerably more manageable than a sheaf of photocopied paper resources. It fits extremely well with the 'Connecting the Learning' phase of the Accelerated Learning Cycle, which many schools are using to good effect. As Alistair Smith (1996) notes:

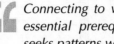 *Connecting to what the learner already knows and understands is an essential prerequisite for accelerating learning. The brain constantly seeks patterns which are already known and understood and its capacity to recognize and learn new patterns. Leslie Hart* [an expert author on brain based learning] *said of this propensity, "recognition of patterns accounts largely for what is called insight, and facilitates transfer of learning to new situations or needs, which may be called creativity."*

The website is an ever present map which, with a few clicks, allows students to see where they are going, where they have been and where their work fits into the wider programme of work they are doing. The ease of movement around the site makes it relatively easy for students to search for connections and make comparisons between Aztecs, Vikings and Victorians. A quick look at a few Aztec images is enough to bring the memories flooding back for many students, whereas a 'Remember when we did the Aztecs?' question is more likely to produce rows of furrowed brows.

The scale and ambition of what students are being asked to do, as well as the use of appropriate technical language, is a reminder to all of us as teachers of the importance of having high expectations, and the ability of students of all ages and abilities to achieve these expectations given the appropriate support.

The intent by teachers to involve their students so heavily in the evolution of the site is evident by the following quote from the 'about us' page: *'We didn't want our site to mention Governors, Ofsted etc .... we want our children to USE it to access the internet whether they have a computer at home or not.'* Here again, we see the technology being used to help build what is described in the Critical Skills Programme as a 'collaborative learning community'.

Snaith Primary School web page on the Aztecs

WEBSITE   Fig 1.2   http://home.freeuk.net/elloughton13/mexico.htm

Scroll down and click on
'The Market' icon

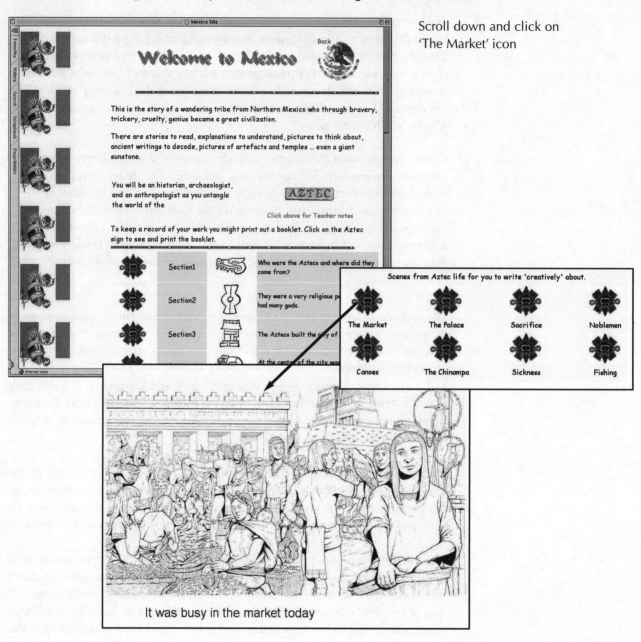

*The opening page of the Snaith Primary School resources on the Aztecs,
and one of the creative writing prompts.*

Example 2: What were shops like a long time ago?

WEBSITE   http://www.j-sainsbury.co.uk/museum/ks1frameset.htm

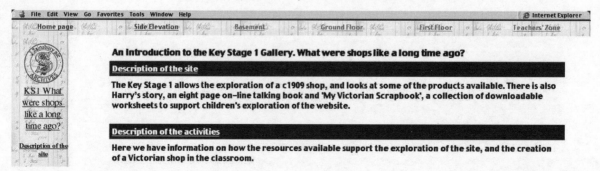

If you found the Snaith website a bit intimidating then you're probably not alone! However, take comfort from the fact that there are lots of good teachers out there creating resources which are no less engaging and valid, but are a bit simpler. Some of these teachers were lucky enough to bump into archivists at the Sainsbury's archives, and so we ended up with excellent resources like those in example two and figure 1.3.

Fig 1.3   Resources on Harry's Day from the Sainsbury's archive website

Click on 'Downloading resources' and then on the second Word document icon 'Harryact.doc'

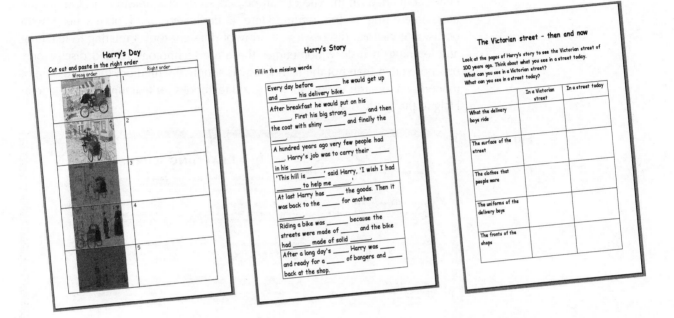

It's worth noting the value of the word processor in these activities. The technology makes it easy to drag and drop the visual images again and again until students are satisfied with their results. The word processor provides an incentive to try and re-try with the text based activities because it is so easy to revisit work and correct errors. These writing frameworks are familiar tools in primary schools for scaffolding students' work, and they are good activities. In this instance the word processor does not create a new activity, it simply extends an existing approach by giving students more control of the resource.

All of these activities are also ideal for whiteboard use. From an historical point of view, it's worth noting that this is real history. Harry really did exist, and these exercises are based on original sources and recorded interviews with Harry. We have pay slips, job descriptions and a range of other documents that underpin this fun activity. Thus, we have an accessible way of introducing young students to concepts of sequence and order, the value of original sources, and a sense of how the past was similar to, and different from, today.

WEBSITE

Example 3: SchoolHistory.co.uk

http://www.schoolhistory.co.uk

Teachers
Forums
Students

SchoolHistory.co.uk

Home | Links | Lessons | Resources | Diagrams | Games | Quizzes | Teachers | Help | Search

You need Flash 6 to view this site properly. It is one free, quick and easy download away.

This website is an extraordinary achievement as it is the work of one teacher. A quick glimpse at figure 1.4 shows the amazing range of resources which are either contained on the site or can be accessed via a link from it. One of the most interesting is the forum. Here a dedicated band of teachers, with occasional visitors, discuss a vast array of different topics relating to teaching and learning in history. Sometimes these are technology related discussions, but more often than not the technology is simply the medium for discussion of more down to earth issues, such as good textbooks for teaching about General Haig at the Battle of the Somme.

Fig 1.4

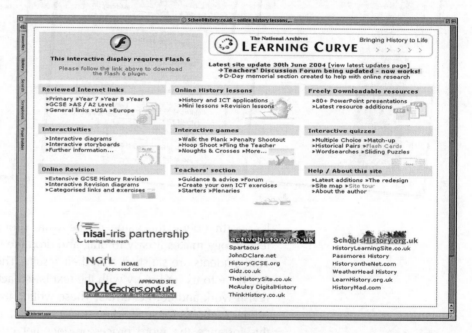

As with the previous examples, this website is driven by learning. It is designed to use technology to provide resources, games, activities and ready to use presentations which all help students to engage with and better understand history. They can consult interactive diagrams and call up a range of resources to help with revision. They can go to one section of the site and get help with homework. Tellingly, the motto in this area is 'Help – but not done for you'. Perhaps the most amazing thing about this website is the fact that it links to more than ten other sites which are also created and run by teachers, with just as many creative ideas and just as much commitment to student learning – a triumph of reality over rhetoric!

Example 4: Snapshot Britain c1900

As with the primary examples, there is no need for a history department to feel inadequate for not having an all singing, all dancing website. There are plenty of valid, challenging and engaging activities, which students can do with relatively simple resources. A pair of teachers in London (one a history specialist, the other an ICT specialist) developed this next exercise, in figure 1.5, to look at conditions in Victorian Britain around 1900. They started with extracts from Robert Tressell's book, *The Ragged Trousered Philanthropists.* It describes how hard life was for the poorest working people in the early 1900s. Students were then asked to see how far the statements made in this extract were supported by census data. They were encouraged to think critically about what the data could do. They were also encouraged to think hard about the relative validity of different types of source material. Needless to say, such high level thinking needed some support, which was provided in a writing frame which students used to reflect not only on what they had learned but also how they had learned it. They also reached high levels of attainment in ICT by considering the strengths and limitations of the software they were using.

Fig 1.5   **Framework used to help students reflect on their learning in the investigation into life in Britain c1900**

Writing frame – Living Standards in London 1891

The hypothesis I was investigating was…

The 1891 census helps historians draw conclusions about the different standards of living in Greenwich and Tower Hamlets. The indicators of a poor standard of living are…

The indicators of a high standard of living are…

My research shows that in Greenwich there are…

While in Tower Hamlets the percentage of … is…

This suggests that… and …

The reason why I think this is because…

On the other hand not all the evidence was as clear-cut.

Evidence to support there being similar standards of living can be seen in pie chart/bar chart…

This shows that the proportion/percentage of…. whereas the proportion of…. is only…

This suggests…

Overall therefore the evidence seems to show that in the areas of…

Life in… was much worse/better than life in …

Using ViewPoint software was helpful in arriving at my conclusions because…

However, I need to be cautious about my conclusions because the data set does not give complete information about standards of living. Other aspects of standards of living that I need to research further are…

The types of evidence that I need to do this are…

Inspiration and aspiration – bridging the gap between rhetoric and reality

I have deliberately chosen these four examples because in one sense they illustrate extremes. Examples 1 and 3 (Snaith Primary School and SchoolHistory) are the result of intense dedication of time and resources to the creation of an exciting and comprehensive resource. I have no hesitation in saying that I find them inspirational. Examples 2 and 4 (Sainsbury's archive and writing frame) are perhaps a little more down to earth but are resources which most teachers could aspire to use even if they are only beginning to use ICT in their teaching. More to the point, they could use these resources with relatively little training or ICT expertise. Even more to the point, having used resources such as these a few times, most teachers could reasonably aspire to customizing them so that they meet their needs more precisely. Better still, they might create similar versions of these resources for different topic areas. The basic process of examining Harry's day in example 2 might easily be adapted to use with a day in the life of a typical Roman. The process of analysing data in example 4 might be replicated by students looking at Domesday Book to see whether the impact of the Norman Conquest described in medieval chronicles fits with the Domesday data for a locality.

All of these 'mights' and 'coulds' may seem a bit provisional to the average busy teacher. I believe one reason for the concerns that many teachers have about the use of ICT is the immense pressure being put on them to use ICT without a comparable level of research, trialling and professional development to accompany this pressure. Successive Ofsted reports into history in primary and secondary schools point to the potential contribution of ICT. However, they also point to the need for clear objectives, guidance for students and the need to make learning and achievement possible for the full range of abilities.

In other words, there are still many issues that teachers are grappling with in 'normal' history teaching. Getting to grips with ICT needs to be seen in this wider context. Getting to grips with ICT in the teaching of history also needs to be seen in the wider context of what responsibility, if any, teachers feel they have to make explicit the learning which is taking place in other areas, such as literacy or ICT. In the secondary classroom it is much more likely that the priority will be historical knowledge and understanding. Despite this, the rest of this book will hopefully show that good activities which prioritize learning in history are not incompatible with achievement in other areas. In the primary classroom a similar balance must be found. As a historian, I am encouraged by the extent to which teachers in primary schools are teaching history for its own sake and value, and using ICT purely for its ability to enhance learning and enjoyment in history. That said, history is an excellent vehicle for cross-curricular work. The Primary National Strategy encourages teachers to look for opportunities to promote excellence and enjoyment and to be creative. The examples shown earlier in this chapter surely meet this criteria.

As a history teacher, this is the moment of truth. Where do you currently belong on this continuum and where would you like to be, say, five years from now?

I am interested in the occasional use of ICT resources in history lessons.	I want to use existing resources, create my own and use them on a fairly regular basis.	I want to build a programme of history lessons which is entirely based around electronic resources.
I am interested only in the progress my students make in historical knowledge and understanding.	I am interested in developing other areas such as literacy and ICT as well as historical knowledge and understanding.	I am prepared to make a big commitment to developing other areas such as literacy and ICT as well as historical knowledge and understanding in order to justify extensive access to computer equipment for my students.

It is worth thinking in these longer-term timescales and remembering that the television took some years to become an accepted part of the pedagogical arsenal for primary and secondary school teachers. Even today, Ofsted reports comment on when a television programme is used particularly effectively, implying that there are occasions when it is used less effectively than it might be. At the same time, it must be admitted that the two resources are not entirely comparable. Both certainly require clear objectives to achieve maximum effect. However, it would be naive to suggest that the introduction and effective use of ICT in history is as simple as the use of television. There are many contextual factors involving access to equipment, educational priorities and, above all, teacher experience and expertise that impinge upon the effective use of ICT. In the next chapter, we are going to examine some of the factors that may help you to plan and make decisions about where you go from here.

Chapter 2

A cunning plan? The learning package

In this section you will discover:

■ The problems of getting enough access to computers may not be entirely solved by having more computers. Their organization and use is just as important.

■ ICT resources can play a key role in supporting tasks and activities which address a range of preferred learning styles.

■ Teachers of history need to be more aware of the ways in which the aims of their subject are compatible with the aims of teachers of ICT.

■ There are strong forces that favour closer links between history and ICT and provide incentives for history teachers to explore ways of embedding ICT in history practice.

■ Teachers of history need to think carefully about how and why they are using ICT and how it will enhance learning in history.

▌The learning package

At a national level there is a problem in making effective use of ICT in history (and all other subjects). Ultimately, the answer to this lies in thoughtful, joined up planning by individual teachers, departments and entire schools.

I have termed this planning the learning package. It is in no way an official term, more a useful way of thinking. It keeps the focus on learning, and how ICT enhances learning. The word 'package' serves to remind us that effective learning using ICT is indeed a package, but it is not a software package. It is a package which consists of intelligent and thoughtful planning, good teaching and sensible combinations of resources, some of which are electronic and some are not. The learning package could be used as a method of exploring how best to make use of ICT resources in programmes such as the Accelerated Learning Cycle or Critical Skills.

Key features of the Accelerated Learning Cycle	Examples of how using ICT in history fits with the Accelerated Learning Cycle
Connection phase	ICT can be a powerful tool for connecting different aspects of historical study in students' minds. The internet provides access to a wide range of multimedia source material, which can be used to trigger memories of previous work and/or to get students thinking about similarities and differences between periods.
Activation phase	A key element of student activities in schools which use accelerated learning approaches is that the input of information should be accessible to a range of different preferred learning styles. The most common shorthand for this is the VAK (visual, auditory, kinesthetic) approach. ICT resources allow students to access historical source material in forms which range from the written text source, through oral and video resources to spatial reconstructions using virtual reality. Using data handling it is even possible to make history accessible to those whose preferred learning style is logical and mathematical.
Demonstration phase	ICT is an output (authoring) tool as well as an input resource. The very nature of ICT militates in favour of students demonstrating their understanding of historical topics in multimedia products.
Consolidation phase	ICT, particularly the word processor, is a tool for processing information. Reviewing, reorganizing, summarizing are all excellent tools for helping students to embed their short-term learning into the long-term memory. ICT applications can help with the laborious donkey work of listing, rewriting, reorganizing and reproducing information. The intellectual processes remain the same.

Key features of the Critical Skills Programme	Examples of how using ICT in history fits with the Critical Skills Programme
Specific curriculum targets	Exploring and defining potential outcomes and progression routes in history and ICT can clarify and enhance student understanding of what they are trying to achieve.
Collaborative learning community	Demonstrating understanding by creating, publishing and presenting ICT based materials involves collaborative working. Online communication such as video or email conferencing can build worldwide communities.
Problem-based challenges	ICT can present a wide range of 'helpful problems' which are in effect opportunities to set challenges to students that they will enjoy tackling. With ICT, these could range from the location of relevant information to the construction of sophisticated multimedia products.
Meaningful context	Building a connection between history and ICT can help to increase students' awareness of the relevance of both areas to today's world in areas such as information management and tourism.
The pupil cycle	Electronic products have a particular appeal, especially to peer groups. A culture in which students regularly create and publish such resources can help to create an environment in which students are encouraged to look at each others' work.
The teacher cycle	As with almost all types of work, teacher modelling is vital if students are to understand what is required from them. ICT provides a range of flexible tools to help them model students' work and even to provide pro forma pieces of work which students reshape themselves.
Transferring and connecting	The use of the computer interface and devices such as hyperlinks in presentations, web pages and other documents can help teachers and students build and view connections between different aspects of their learning in history.

Of course, many of these approaches are already being used in schools, whether they are part of Critical Skills or accelerated learning schemes or not. In many respects they are all rather obvious to teachers who have a sense of what good teaching and learning looks like. On the other hand, much anecdotal evidence suggests that using ICT often gets in the way of effective teaching and learning instead of complementing or enhancing it. Let's look first at some of the issues that cause these problems.

Access to computers: Where does the real problem lie?

If you ask an audience of secondary history teachers the primary reason cited as to why relatively little effective (or even ineffective) use of ICT is made in history, the answer is lack of access to computers. The usual reason for this seems to be the block booking of computer suites for courses in business studies or ICT taught discretely. In primary schools, the issue is generally more a management issue, specifically the best way to get maximum use from a small number of machines in a classroom.

At a superficial level, therefore, it might seem that more hardware is the obvious answer to this fundamental problem. However, when we think more deeply it raises questions. Have the same assumptions ever been made about other resources such as television programmes or books as have been made about ICT? Has any other resource been so effectively divorced from the pedagogy deployed with the resource? The following experience, noted by Terry Haydn and Christine Counsell (2003), is highly illuminating:

> The failure of policy makers, resource managers or school leaders to foster, analyse and use their own teachers' professional knowledge about teaching and learning may well be a reason for the frustrating slowness with which this transformation (i.e. ICT transforming learning) is coming about. In the early days of using computers in history lessons during the 1970s and 1980s, when the history education world was sparsely populated with skilful enthusiasts and influential pioneers, a couple of computers in the classroom was a more typical pattern. There was much to be learned about how teachers deployed these to enrich a particular aspect of historical learning for an individual pupil or a group of pupils. But as the number of computers in schools has expanded, concerns about efficiency and maximizing access have been translated into large suites where 'sole-user access' is the expectation. This goes right against a sensible and flexible integration of ICT with the process of historical enquiry, where a computer is pulled in to serve a data-management, investigational or communication need at a particular stage in the lesson sequence. Pupils then see clearly – and are ultimately able to choose – its role in serving the enquiry 'journey'. When the fifteenth and last of the original City Technology Colleges, John Cabot CTC, was set up in Bristol in 1993, the question of hardware deployment in a relatively ICT-rich environment was a hot agenda item. The humanities faculty's preferred model was 3–4 computers in each classroom for history, geography and RE. This model was used successfully in the early years. The influence here was subject-specific. Influenced by Michael Riley's idea of 'enquiry' (Riley 2000), as a governing idea for planning, and by ideas then circulating about geographical enquiry, the faculty's teachers wanted pupils to learn the value and functions of ICT in context. It became

increasingly hard, however, to defend this deployment. Wouldn't we minimize the time during which computers lay idle (ran the counter argument) if they were all together in dedicated suites where they could be used intensively? This was a clash of two discourses – a managerialist assumption that constant use represented value for money versus a teacher's strong pedagogic judgement that contextualized use and the cultivation of critical expertise in pupils formed a better investment.

The lesson to be drawn from this experience, replicated in many other schools, is that subject teachers need to make the case for an approach to the use of ICT which is driven by pedagogy. In other words, a vision in which ICT supports learning rather than one where the use of ICT forces learning to adapt (some would say contort) itself to make use of ICT.

The perception problem: Linking history with ICT

The next major obstacle to the effective use of ICT is a perception problem. I have been running INSET courses on history and ICT for many years. It is amazing how often history teachers have regarded the phrase 'history and ICT' as a contradiction in terms.

More understandable, but also more damaging, is the fact that this perception is widespread in other subject teachers, and this of course includes ICT co-ordinators. Ignorance of the specialisms of their colleagues is a sad but understandable fact of life in secondary schools. This is not the place to lament this ignorance, but in the case of ICT it is a factor which needs to be addressed because unless the ICT co-ordinator and/or the history department become more aware of the complementary nature of their subjects, then the situation will not improve. Primary colleagues, of course, have the advantage on the secondary specialist in this respect in that they generally teach a wide range of subjects. However, experience seems to show that even primary teachers do not see history as the obvious context for an ICT assignment.

The perceived lack of synergy between history and ICT is something which we all need to work at. In a secondary school the ICT co-ordinator is probably under pressure to integrate at least some ICT into specific subjects. But where will they turn if they do not have a history background? History is much more likely to get its place in the sun if the history department take the time and trouble to explain to the ICT co-ordinator the nature of the subject. It is quite likely that he/she will not be aware of the nature of history as an enquiry based, investigative, discursive, analytical and judgemental discipline. The average non-specialist ICT co-ordinator or non-specialist (in history) primary school teacher may be similarly unaware of the nature of history as a discipline, and also the vast wealth of high quality free resources to support history. History is probably the best supported subject in terms of online resources, and not even science can boast a resource as impressive as the National Archives Learning Curve. So history has much to offer in terms of its raw content. The discipline of history also has huge amounts to offer ICT in terms of analytical processes, critical thinking and thoughtful presentation, which are such critical ingredients of ICT.

▌ The disappointment factor: Teacher knowledge, experience and expertise

Another factor which has probably held back effective use of ICT in history is that on the occasions when teachers have been able to use ICT the results have been less impressive than they hoped for, or have actually been a negative experience for teachers and/or students. Sometimes these negative outcomes have been the result of technical difficulties – the educational equivalent of the insurers' term 'Act of God' in the sense that the difficulties could not be predicted. More often, however, technical difficulties have simply exaggerated problems of planning and preparation.

One example recounted to me during an INSET exemplifies this. A teacher (and ICT enthusiast) told me that he had managed to secure three precious lessons with a Year 8 group in the computer room and was planning to tackle some data handling. The experience turned sour because the students were unable to use the data handling software and the history teacher spent most of the three lessons teaching students the basics of the software. At one level this might be seen as an example of the hassle factor in using ICT which negates any worth it might have. That said, the history teacher was gracious enough to admit that he had not consulted with his colleagues in ICT as to what Year 8 students had done in data handling, and further admitted that some liaison of this sort could have avoided the problems encountered.

Technical difficulties aside, there is no doubt that in both primary and secondary history the use of ICT had sometimes been disappointing because our planning and pedagogy with regard to history has not been sharp enough. The use of ICT tends to magnify problems like this. The classic example is something which I have called 'Encarta syndrome', referring to the Microsoft multimedia encyclopedia. In this example, the teacher asks the students 'to find out about' some topic or historical figure, without giving any clear guidance. The result is invariably that the student uses Encarta or a similar CD-ROM or website and simply prints out the information. It is then presented in triumph as 'my work', despite the fact that little studying of the topic has actually taken place. The student has not read the relevant material but has simply found it. Such an approach by a student would not be tolerated in the use of any other resource and it should not be tolerated in the use of ICT.

WEBSITE

It is not difficult to get around such problems as Encarta syndrome. As Ofsted reports suggest (www.ofsted.gov.uk/reports/), the key element is careful planning. First and foremost, the aims in terms of historical knowledge and understanding must be clear. If the teacher, primary or secondary, is unclear about what they want students to achieve in terms of historical knowledge and understanding then there is little chance that the use of ICT will correct this. Secondly, the teacher needs to have a clear vision of how the use of ICT will help the students to achieve the aims that the lesson is trying to achieve. If you cannot state clearly why you are using ICT in a particular context, then you simply should not use it at all.

The Ofsted *Subject Reports 1999-2000: history* (2000) summed up the position very succinctly:

 Departments make effective use of ICT more often when they show good awareness of the range of applications of ICT in history, have them built into the scheme of work, and exploit these regularly for progressive use of research, analysis and communication.

There are some important points in this comment. Teachers need to be aware of the range of applications and, by implication, the uses of these applications in history classrooms. It is all too tempting to interpret 'applications' as referring to subject specific software which will somehow do the job of making students think and learn. There certainly are history specific resources, but these are usually sources of information. As most teachers know, and so few politicians seem willing to hear, access to information is the start of the learning process, not the end. Most history teachers have found that the really beneficial effects in terms of student learning have come in a combination of content resources and what is called productivity software – word-processing, data handling and presentation software.

Let's revisit the Encarta syndrome previously described. This could be turned into a meaningful activity relatively easily. Instead of asking students to find out about Elizabeth I, we can sharpen the focus. Our task could be revised to ask some Year 6 students, or perhaps Year 8, to write a short biography of Elizabeth I for students younger than themselves. They have to decide, say, what five things every person of a particular age should really know about Elizabeth I.

A focus such as this immediately gives purpose to the task and requires students to process the available information and create their own new product. ICT is playing a role in that the information is from an ICT resource. ICT could play a further role by asking students to use a word processor with the Encarta article. They could copy the article into a word processor file and use the word count function to see how many words were in the article. They could then be given the task of reducing the word count. Clearly the length of the original article and the extent by which they must reduce the text will vary according to the age and ability of students. In the case of Elizabeth I on Encarta, the full article might be rather daunting, but the outline table of events of her life could be used as the main source of information instead of the article. The main point here is that the word processor actually facilitates effective reading. It is so easy to cut, rearrange and edit that the functionality of the word processor adds real value. The final edited text could be re-presented again as a series of bullet points in a presentation.

This is just one example of an activity in which valid learning in history is taking place, and the use of ICT actively promotes and supports the learning. Most of the rest of this book is focused on examples such as this. However, before we get to these examples we need to consider a few more context factors.

▌Factors favouring closer links between history and ICT

Statutory requirements to use ICT in history

WEBSITE

It is easy to forget that the national curriculum for history KS2 and KS3 clearly sets out a requirement to use ICT in the course of the history programme of study (www.nc.uk.net). In the folders below, roman text denotes a statutory requirement while the italic text denotes a recommendation.

Nat. Curr. ⟍ Ofsted

Organization and communication
Historical enquiry
4. Pupils should be taught:
   a) how to find out about the events, people and changes studied from an appropriate range of sources of information, including ICT-based sources *[for example, documents, printed sources, CD-ROMS, databases, pictures and photographs, music, artefacts, historic buildings and visits to museums, galleries and sites]*

Organization and communication
5. Pupils should be taught to:
   c) communicate their knowledge and understanding of history in a variety of ways *[for example, drawing, writing, by using ICT]*.

National curriculum for history in England KS2

Nat. Curr. ⟍ Ofsted

Historical enquiry
4. Pupils should be taught to:
   a) identify, select and use a range of appropriate sources of information including oral accounts, documents, printed sources, the media, artefacts, pictures, photographs, music, museums, buildings and sites, and ICT-based sources as a basis for independent historical enquiries

Organization and communication
5. Pupils should be taught to:
   c) communicate their knowledge and understanding of history, using a range of techniques, including spoken language, structured narratives, substantiated explanations and the use of ICT.

National curriculum for history in England KS3

This statutory requirement might be used by teachers to gently remind their managers and possibly ICT colleagues that history is a suitable vehicle for developing student skills in ICT and that ICT can enhance teaching and learning in virtually all subjects, not just a narrow range of technical or vocational subjects.

History's vocational relevance in the specific context of ICT

Reflection on programmes such as the Critical Skills Programme suggests that many students look with fresh eyes on tasks and even whole subjects, if the connection between what they are doing and 'real life' is clear. History often faces a particularly bad press among students in this particular area. It is up to us as history teachers to remind students that history has a direct relevance to the world of work. The indirect claims are often made – the skills of research, analysis, evaluation, presentation – for history's vocational relevance. These are utterly valid claims, and it is no coincidence that a high proportion of lawyers, accountants, journalists and the like studied history to degree level. But not all students will become graduate historians. For the majority, history is also an excellent vehicle for developing the skills at the sharp end of the information economy, which is becoming a dominant feature in the work landscape.

Let's look at two apparently contrasting scenarios. In the first scenario, a call centre representative is asked to provide a customer with a quote for insurance which best suits the customer's needs. The representative has to search the databases of a number of different insurance companies for the best quote. In this instance, the best quote is not necessarily the cheapest as the customer has very specific requirements. Therefore, in the course of the enquiry it is likely that the call centre representative will:

➡ evaluate what the customer's question is really asking

➡ locate sources of information to answer the question

➡ assess the relevance of information for the enquiry

➡ assess the value and reliability of information for the particular enquiry

➡ reach a balanced judgement based on the available evidence.

In the second scenario, a teacher might ask students to use data handling software to interrogate census data from a particular locality and investigate whether claims made in a local newspaper of the time about immigrants were actually supported by the data. In this instance, students would have to tackle all of the processes listed above for scenario 1. What's more, they would be using the same type of software and data structure to do this.

A final, and equally telling, point on the vocational relevance of history in the context of ICT is the importance of history as a leisure pursuit. A huge number of television programmes, movies, computer games, tourist attractions, museums and heritage sites either use aspects of history or draw on history for their core appeal. Genealogy is becoming a very popular hobby and is a major presence on the world wide web. The relevance of history in this new media age might encompass a wide range of areas such as:

➡ Marketing a site – for example, a building, a street, a landscape – on the basis of its history: this is increasingly a web based skill as more and more bookings are made online.

➡ Designing and developing booking systems for historic attractions: this could be done for other types of attractions, but since heritage is such a huge element of the leisure and tourism market it seems as logical to use the history context as any other.

➡ Designing and writing websites that support television programmes and movies with an historical theme.

➡ Researching television programmes/movies and/or events, such as re-enactments. One of the most critical elements in reconstructions is to establish an authentic sense of period and avoid anachronisms.

➡ Designing and writing interpretative resources for historic sites or museums, such as touch screen information devices.

Ofsted and the issue of teaching and learning in ICT

The initial rush to simply get computers into schools with relatively little consideration about the best way to use them appears to be over. Historically, the focus has been on the quality of teaching and learning in ICT lessons, however, there is now a tighter focus on how we can get the best value from these machines in terms of learning.

Ofsted reports in this area have been generally critical, for a wide and complex range of reasons. One of these reasons must be, however, that the poor beleaguered teacher in charge of ICT is almost certainly a non-specialist, whether in primary or secondary schools. Another reason is that the vast array of skills which students must master to progress in ICT require contexts to have any meaning. Thus, an exercise in demonstrating presentation skills is pretty meaningless unless the presentation is actually about something! It is here that many educationalists feel that individual subjects may be able to really enhance the teaching and learning of ICT by marrying their specialist contexts with the requirements of the ICT curriculum and the capabilities of hardware and software. That said, Ofsted reports also seem to suggest that there is still a lot of work to do before this is done universally and effectively.

Nat. Curr. | **Ofsted**

There has been a small improvement in the resources for history, including the extent to which information and communication technology (ICT) is available and used.

Ofsted subject reports 2002/03, history in primary schools, February 2004

Nat. Curr. | **Ofsted**

Although many schools have made great strides in the teaching of ICT capability, the use of ICT frequently does not have sufficient impact on **teaching and learning in other subjects**. For such integration to take place teachers need to develop their confidence beyond basic ICT skills to identify the gains in teaching and learning that a particular application brings to subject work. In one school, for example, a range of applications was noted as teachers branched out from their teaching of ICT only in ICT lessons:

Some classes use ICT to help writing in literacy lessons, for example using a text to improve punctuation or vocabulary, or printing their poems about Van Gogh and displaying these attractively with the paintings. Pupils in several classes made graphs and charts to present information or to solve problems in mathematics lessons. Pupils in Year 5 used a spreadsheet to compare the diameter and circumference of a circle, and then used this to predict the results for larger circles. Older pupils used a spreadsheet to record and predict their science results. These tools helped pupils to see patterns in their data and improve their understanding.

Ofsted subject reports 2002/03, Information and communication technology in primary schools, February 2004

Nat. Curr. | **Ofsted**

There have been some improvements in the use of information and communication technology (ICT), but in one third of schools this is unsatisfactory.

Ofsted subject reports 2002/03, history in secondary schools, February 2004

Nat. Curr. | **Ofsted**

Where attainment in Key Stage 3 is good, pupils are making choices about the best ICT tools to use and applying these appropriately to a variety of tasks. They have a sense of their intended audience and are guided by teachers to assess critically their own and others' work and make appropriate improvements. However, there are still too many lessons where ICT learning takes place in unimaginative contexts and pupils have insufficient opportunity to apply their ICT learning to studies in other subjects.

Discrete ICT courses and the application of ICT in other subjects
Inspection evidence continues to point to a mixed approach of discrete and cross-curricular ICT as delivering the optimum balance for pupils. However, while there has been some improvement this year in the extent and quality of ICT work in other subjects in Key Stages 3 and 4, the proportion of such lessons that are unsatisfactory or poor remains high and is around one in three in some subjects.

Reliance only on cross-curricular uses of ICT to develop pupils' capability is without doubt a difficult option. While a few schools succeed in this approach, many do not, because of the demands made on curriculum planning, co-ordination and staff development. Often, the use of ICT in other subjects does not extend or reinforce pupils' ICT capability.

The use of ICT is not guaranteed to enhance teaching and learning in other subjects. For example, the production of multimedia presentations may enable pupils to reapply the skills learned in ICT lessons, but if they focus on too narrow a range of learning, this may not be a good investment of time in the context of the subject. ICT-based learning works best where it is led by the learning objectives of the subject being taught.

Ofsted subject reports 2002/03, Information and communication technology in secondary schools, February 2004

Developments in teaching and learning in ICT

There have been many initiatives and government sponsored programmes designed to remedy some of the main problems which Ofsted reports have highlighted. In the primary sector, one of the most important developments has sets out a requirement to use ICT in the course of the history programme of been the schemes of work (www.standards.dfes.gov.uk/schemes3/) for ICT and indeed history and every other national curriculum subject. In history, the schemes of work have been used widely and effectively. The schemes of work for ICT have also raised standards in ICT. On the other hand they have not had a major impact on integration of ICT resources in such a way that they enhance students' learning.

WEBSITE

This is really where the onus falls on the teacher responsible for history rather than the colleague with responsibility for ICT. In simple terms, the ICT schemes need to be looked at and considered in terms of how and where history might provide the context for effective learning in both ICT and history to take place. A quick glance at some of the primary schemes of work for ICT suggests immediate possibilities.

ICT scheme of work	Possible history contexts
1.b) Using a word bank	Students selecting words which describe particular famous historical figures.
2.a) Writing stories: communicating information using text	The activities in this unit include labelling objects; completing missing word activities; creating lists. These approaches could be applied to Aztec objects; a story from Ancient Greece; a list of ways in which Victorians were different from us.
2.c) Finding information/ 2.e) Questions and Answers/ 3.c) Introduction to databases	It is hard to think of an historical context which would not use this skill! One such might be the use of local census information and/or Ordnance Survey maps to see how a local area has changed.
4.a) Writing for different audiences	Students might write a script for a television programme which could be a dramatic reconstruction or a present-day documentary.
6.a) Multimedia presentation	Students could research a local historic site and prepare an introductory presentation for visitors to the site.
6.d) Using the internet to search large databases and interpret information	Shipping or other business records might be analysed to investigate which trades were prosperous at different times.

In the secondary sector, the schemes of work have been superseded to some extent by the advent of the KS3 Framework for ICT – part of the government's KS3 Strategy. The same basic principle applies as in the primary sector, however. Few history teachers will baulk at the objectives of the KS3 Framework for ICT which include:

➡ Finding things out;
  ➡ using data and information sources
  ➡ searching and selecting
  ➡ organizing and investigating.

➡ Exchanging and sharing information;
  ➡ fitness for purpose
  ➡ refining and presenting information
  ➡ communicating.

In 2003–2004, as part of a government initiative, the Historical Association worked in partnership with the DfES on a project called 'ICT Across the Curriculum'. The aim was to map the requirements of the KS1–2 national curriculum for ICT and the KS3 Framework for ICT and to consider subject specific contexts in which ICT requirements could easily and appropriately be met. The framework on page 34 (figure 2.1) shows just a small sample of the mapping that was carried out for the secondary project. It should be stressed that the pre-eminent requirement in this exercise was that the quality of learning in history or the other subjects should not be compromised or distorted by the use of ICT. In areas where there was no natural compatibility between history and ICT (such as certain aspects of control technology) the mapping exercise stated this clearly. In addition to this mapping, a number of sample lessons with supporting resources were produced. The entire package (one might say a learning package!) was published on CD-ROM and distributed freely to schools.

Fig 2.1   Extract from the ICTAC history materials

Subject commentary

Opportunities to apply and develop ICT capability in history

Overarching statement

4.   Pupils should be taught to:
   a) identify, select and use a range of appropriate sources of information as a basis for independent historical enquiries.
   b) evaluate the sources used, select and record information relevant to the enquiry and reach conclusions.

Commentary

Information is the raw material of history, and pupils need to be critical in its use. They also develop skills relating to the type of data source – paintings are very different sources to cartoons or speeches, for example. As they progress from Year 7 to Year 9 pupils will be expected to become much more critical in their use of sources.

Example(s)

(1) Year 7 pupils might be asked to look at a website that illustrates the Bayeux Tapestry. They are asked to tell the story of the Norman Invasion from the tapestry. By asking them whose point of view is the tapestry from, and whose point of view is missing, pupils will begin to see the limitations of using just one type of evidence. This could be taken further by asking them to look, for instance, at the Anglo-Saxon Chronicle and to consider how different a picture is given by a text source.

(2) Year 8 pupils could be asked to study the Armada. By giving them a Spanish interpretation of the events they should be challenged to consider viewpoint, and its importance in reading and writing history.

(3) Year 9 pupils could, when studying the Cold War, be given two points of view – one source suggesting that the Cold War was the Americans' fault; the other that it was the Russians' fault – and asked to produce an account of the Cold War. Such emotive websites are easily found!

Key concepts with ICT framework objectives

Using data and information sources

Year 7	Year 8	Year 9
Understand that different forms of information – text, graphics, sound, numeric data and symbols – can be combined to create meaning and impact. Identify the purpose of an information source (e.g. to present facts or opinions, to advertise, publicize or entertain) and whether it is likely to be biased. Identify what information is relevant to a task. Understand how someone using an information source could be misled by missing or inaccurate information.	Understand how the content and style of an information source affect its suitability for particular purposes, by considering: – its mix of fact, opinion and material designed to advertise, publicize or entertain; – the viewpoints it offers; – the clarity, accessibility and plausibility of the material. Devise and apply criteria to evaluate how well various information sources will support a task. Justify the use of particular information sources to support an investigation or presentation.	Select information sources and data systematically for an identified purpose by: – judging the reliability of the information sources; – identifying possible bias due to sampling methods; – collecting valid, accurate data efficiently; – recognizing potential misuse of collected data.

New technologies: whiteboards

In the early 2000s, one technology is becoming increasingly common and relatively easily accessible – the interactive whiteboard. It is important to remember that the whiteboard is one element of a trio of resources. The other two are the data projector and the laptop or desktop computer. The value of these resources is widely recognized in primary and secondary schools and there are many examples of students being enthused and motivated by skilful teachers making imaginative use of them. Whiteboards appear to be impacting in two main ways. Firstly, they offer an extra dimension to the traditional array of methods used by good classroom teachers. Secondly, whiteboards offer the opportunity to make use of ICT resources when only one machine is available. This could be through teacher led presentation or student presentations. It might be through whole-class feedback on a particular exercise. For example, students might have been asked to select points from a text (a paper handout) which are relevant to a particular issue. The whiteboard can then be used to show which sections students feel are relevant or important. A great deal of time and resources have been invested by government, school managers and teachers in making the best use of whiteboards. There is some evidence of commercial publishers also looking for the best ways to produce material to maximize the impact of this new technology. Figure 2.2 below shows material from a new resource from Nelson Thornes publishers, which supports the Empires and Citizens series. The textbooks in this series are supported by a CD-ROM that allows users to access the images and sources in the text. It also contains a substantial number of animations which help to engage students with the text but also extends the reach of the textbook in areas such as animated maps. A static map in a book cannot convey effectively the one thing it truly aims to covey – progress and movement. An animated map with voice-over commentary can do this, and is exceptionally powerful when used on a whiteboard with a teacher pausing the presentation at the ideal moments. Most of the major book publishers are now developing resources such as these to accompany their textbooks, and the main resource in mind is one which helps the teacher to get the most from the whiteboard.

Fig 2.2 Screens from the *Empires and Citizens* CD-ROM published by Nelson Thornes. A click on the map on the virtual book page brings up the animated map in the second screen

CD-ROM Ch2/Islamic conquests animation

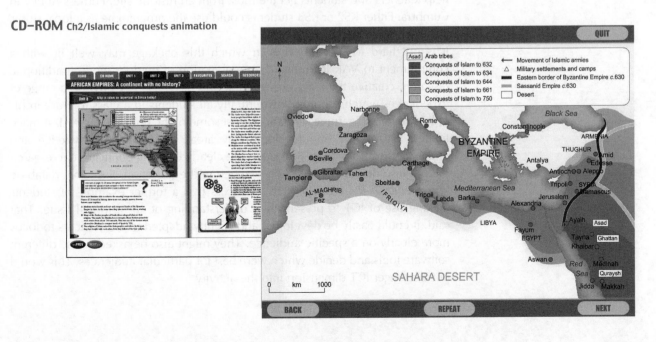

For primary and secondary teachers of history, the key issue is the same as with other aspects of ICT. Teachers need to become aware of how the whiteboard can and does enhance the students' experience of history. There are many ways in which the ability to project electronic material in the classroom will be valuable in history. An inspiring introduction might now be enhanced by an arresting visual image, an animation, an excerpt from a movie. Analysis of a difficult image such as a political cartoon could be tackled by circling and labelling key features of the cartoon which betray its message and possible bias.

Structuring an approach: The learning package

To recap, there are lots of obstacles that militate against the effective use of ICT in history, but on the other hand, there are also lots of factors that are working in our favour.

At this point, the most difficult question for most history teachers is where to start. This is where the notion of the learning package becomes useful. To reiterate, the learning package proposed here is not a software package (such as a CD-ROM or website) that allows you to say you are doing some ICT in history. The learning package combines structured activities which might well use several different software applications at different points of a broad historical enquiry.

It is almost certain to use a range of other resources such as textbooks, television programmes and fieldwork. Wherever possible, the learning package should ideally be developed in collaboration with colleagues responsible for ICT. In this way many practical issues such as the allocations of rooms, equipment, time and so on, may be more easily addressed. More importantly, collaboration between history and ICT colleagues maximizes the opportunities for a professional discourse in which both disciplines learn more about one another and a real understanding develops about how each can help to promote effective learning in the other.

Figure 2.3 shows an example of a learning package which was worked out to help teachers and students get the most from an historic site, Furness Abbey in Cumbria. Either KS2 or KS3 students could use the programme as a local study.

It is not hard to see the ways in which this package may well fit with a commitment to VAK learning. The combination of outdoor work, 'traditional' research, creative thinking, presentation and of course ICT provide a range of experiences which should allow virtually all students in a class to work in his or her preferred learning style for at least some of the unit. Processes 1–4 make limited use of ICT but develop many areas of historical knowledge and understanding. In process 5 students are clearly carrying out historical research but are also demonstrating good practice in the use of an electronic database (the *Medieval Realms* CD–ROM). Process 6 is a further example of students making use of ICT to present their understanding of an historical issue. That said, it could easily be developed and slightly adapted to ask students to focus more clearly on a specific audience. They might also be asked to use different software tools and decide which were best for particular audiences. This would put a stronger ICT dimension into the activity.

Fig 2.3   A learning package designed to make use of ICT and other resources to promote learning in history

Learning objectives — Pupils learn ...	Process/Activities — Processes	Support/Differentiation	Resources	Outcomes — Pupils demonstrate ability to:
Interpretations can be visual, written or spoken. All based on evidence in some form but it may be interpreted differently.	1. Pupils examine artists' reconstructions of Furness Abbey and record the impressions gained from the reconstructions as a series of key points.	Teacher led, with prompts and recording frameworks.	English Heritage site: Furness Abbey, near Barrow in Furness, Cumbria	Compare and assess relative value of different types of source.
The evidence from which interpretations are produced is not always complete.	2. Pupils are armed with copies of reconstructions and are asked to study the site and look for evidence that the artist used to create reconstructions.	Pupils work in pairs or small groups.	British Library CD-ROM *Medieval Realms*	Assess ways in which evidence can be complementary or contradictory.
Monastic life was 'practical' as well as spiritual – monasteries were important political and economic as well as spiritual institutions.	3. Pupils look for areas of the abbey where there does not appear to be evidence for the reconstructed drawings.	Make this or previous task optional for some pupils.	Digital cameras	Use CD-ROM and other resources to exercise research skills and make judgements as to value and relevance of resource materials.
	4. Pupils use the exhibits in the visitor centre and further research to examine everyday life and work of monks in the abbey.	Recording frameworks with key headings such as Food; Prayer; Income; Learning; Power.	Textbooks	Reflect upon and speculate concerning how a visual interpretation was constructed using only limited evidence.
	5. Pupils use CD-ROM resource containing sources on monasteries to carry out further research into life in monasteries. Particular focus on everyday issues not covered by artist's reconstructions that are primarily focused on the fabric of the building.	Tailor extent of research required and nature of source material to abilities of pupils.	Library resources	Communicate ideas and conclusions using presentation and/or multimedia.
	6. Pupils use presentation or multimedia software to summarize conclusions concerning: i) evidence used by artist ii) areas where evidence used by artist is not clear iii) aspects of everyday life in monasteries not featured in reconstructions iv) suggestions about the influences on the artist in making up for lack of evidence (for example, imagination, other interpretations, other sources, audience and purpose of the reconstruction) v) any other points pupils wish to make.	Allow group presentations for less confident pupils. Tailor limits on length, amount of visual/text material to support or challenge pupils appropriately.	Multimedia presentation software	

Where to go from here?

In summary, the message is that teachers of history who want to use ICT to enhance their students' experience of the subject need to balance the following elements:

➡ clear aims in terms of benefits for teaching and learning in history

➡ clear aims in terms of benefits for teaching and learning in ICT

➡ awareness of the applications and resources needed to achieve these aims

➡ what is realistic in terms of equipment

➡ what is realistic in terms of teacher experience and expertise.

The central element has to be a focus on what the use of ICT might be able to do to enhance learning and enjoyment in history. We need to be very clear about the potential advantages which the use of ICT has to offer. These might be summarized as follows:

➡ The opportunity to support a wide range of different learning styles and student needs.

  ➡ VAK friendly input: The first priority when accessing historical resources in electronic forms must be relevance to the topic. However, the internet and other electronic resources provide such a wealth of information that we can afford to think in terms of the format of the information. We are no longer forced to accept that this text is the only source on topic 'X'. We have the option to look for oral, visual, moving image, virtual reality and a range of other forms.

  ➡ VAK friendly output: Authoring tools are now so easy to use and are packed with powerful features that students can make impressive multimedia packages with relative ease.

  ➡ Self-esteem: ICT resources generally allow information to be searched and used in a variety of ways. Authoring resources allow constant revisions and review. It is possible for students with the lowest self-esteem to feel confident that they can always correct their work and that the end product will still look impressive.

➡ Access to material not available otherwise.

  ➡ There is no shortage of historical material available in electronic form, especially on the internet. The challenge for the history teacher is to use this material intelligently. If a website does little more than a textbook then why not use the textbook? There is plenty of material on the internet that would not be available anywhere else. This includes some of the wilder interpretations of history and also a vast resource of artefacts and objects from the world's museums and archives. Using the internet to access such materials is clearly making effective use of the resource. This theme – which might be summed up as 'why are you using the internet?' – recurs throughout the rest of the book but is dealt with in depth in chapter 5.

➡ Support for analytical processes.

➡ History is most emphatically a subject which develops critical thinking and analysis. The very essence of history is to investigate the causes and consequences of events, the relative importance of different factors or individuals. Software tools, such as word processors and data handling packages, are specifically designed to sift, analyse, redraft, reorganize and present information on different forms. These generic 'productivity' tools have shown themselves to be powerful tools in the hands of skilled teachers by helping students to develop analytical thinking and writing. The value of such tools is explored in chapters 3, 4 and 6.

➡ Opportunities for presentation and communication.

➡ It is easy to forget that the 'C' in ICT stands for communication. Electronic resources offer a wide range of ways in which students can demonstrate their understanding of an historical topic. They might use presentation software to demonstrate their understanding of a visual source or try to convince a developer to give archaeologists on a site more time to carry out their investigations. Teachers and students might exchange perspectives on contentious periods of history through email conferencing software.

➡ Ability to work with a range of media and to understand the process of creating media by creating media products.

➡ ICT has been a major contributory factor in the development of news and entertainment. Equipment such as camcorders and software for creating websites or digital video editing give students opportunities to explore how television programmes and other media are created and even create their own. This is the main focus of chapter 7.

Chapter 3

From vicious Vikings to incisive interpretations

In this section you will discover:

■ The greater part of most history lessons is spent working with text. The word processor is far more than a tool for typing text. It is also an excellent tool for analysing, revising, redrafting and reshaping text.

■ Word processors have many features which encourage students to experiment with text, analysing challenging sources and interpretations and constructing their own views based on these sources.

■ The word processor is probably the most familiar ICT application for teachers and students. It provides excellent opportunities to present students with tasks that offer high levels of challenge but low levels of threat, helping to create the secure learning environment essential to effective learning.

■ Many word processor based activities are equally well suited to work in computer rooms or with one computer and a whiteboard.

■ Tasks which use simple ICT can at the same time develop very high level history.

■ Sources of electronic text are becoming increasingly widely available, making it easier for teachers to use word processor based tasks without an excessive burden of preparation.

▌ Getting started: The value of the word processor

It is easy to be seduced or even overwhelmed by the extraordinary possibilities that the use of ICT offers, whether it be authoring web pages or creating video projects. If you are more of a beginner then the humble word processor has a huge amount to offer the teacher of history in the primary or secondary classroom.

Many teachers, primary and secondary, have experimented with the potential of the word processor to help their students learn in history. The Historical Association has published a number of studies and resources. The most comprehensive of these were in partnership with the National Council for Educational Technology, now called BECTA (British Educational Communications and Technology Agency). From this starting point, much more excellent material has been published in the Historical Association's journals *Teaching History* and *Primary History*.

One of the main reasons for this interest is that the word processor is so much more than a typewriter. In 1998, I went on record in the Historical Association journal *Teaching history*, saying that:

> *The word processor is one of the marvels of the modern age, comparable only to the kitchen blender. This redoubtable machine can effortlessly slice, purée, blend, mix and manipulate that most fundamental of human needs, food. The word processor is not far behind in its contribution to civilization. It can search, annotate, organize, classify, draft, reorganize, redraft and save that fundamental of the historian, the written word. When we consider these processes, and the implicit difficulties they represent for so many of our students, the true power and value of the word processor becomes clear. It is not a typewriter; it is an awesome tool for handling information in written form.*

This is a statement that I am still happy to back, and this chapter's aim is to explore a wide range of historical activities in which the word processor can play a useful role. In many cases the role is not essential but it could be extremely helpful. The key, however, is that these are all historical activities. Many have the potential to improve students' understanding and use of ICT. Some could even be used to introduce ICT skills in the first place. Nevertheless, the emphasis is very much on what is in it for the history teacher.

Studying historical interpretations

A good illustration of how the word processor can really help the history teacher can be found in figure 3.1a. The context for this particular instance is the changing nature of historical thinking about the Vikings. Teachers in primary schools have often been caught in the middle of this intellectual crossfire. They have used some resources with their students which suggest that the Vikings were simply traders and craftsmen. This contradicts everything the parents of some of their students were taught about Vikings and long before concerns of 'political correctness gone mad' were raised.

This is exactly why the issue of historical interpretation was brought into the national curriculum orders for history.

Nat. Curr.	Ofsted

Historical interpretation
3.   Pupils should be taught to recognize that the past is represented and interpreted in different ways, and to give reasons for this.

National curriculum for history in England KS2

Nat. Curr. Ofsted

Historical interpretation
3. Pupils should be taught:
   a) how and why historical events, people, situations and changes have been interpreted in different ways
   b) to evaluate interpretations.

National curriculum for history in England KS3

Vicious Vikings?

The requirement to study interpretations was included in the national curriculum orders so that from time to time students might consider questions such as 'Why are there disagreements about what the Vikings were like?' Before students get to grips with why historical accounts differ, it seems sensible for them to get to grips with how accounts differ. This is important because the perception among many students, and indeed the public at large, is that there is 'a story' of the past. Rarely do they come across the fact that the story is usually hotly contested at any given period in time and that it evolves over time as new evidence emerges – as new historians present new ideas and existing historians review their existing ideas. Here the word processor can play an important role. Figure 3.1a shows an example of a task designed to introduce students to the challenging concept of historical interpretations.

Fig 3.1a   **Using the word processor to study historical interpretation**

CD-ROM Ch3/Vikings Word doc

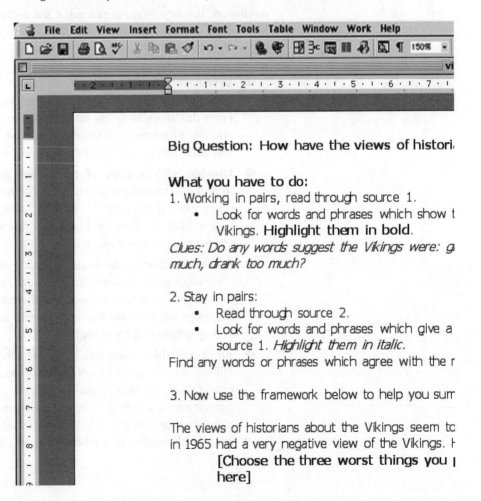

File   Edit   View   Insert   Format   Font   Tools   Table   Window   Work   Help

Big Question: How have the views of histori

What you have to do:
1. Working in pairs, read through source 1.
   • Look for words and phrases which show t
     Vikings. **Highlight them in bold**.
   Clues: Do any words suggest the Vikings were: g
   much, drank too much?

2. Stay in pairs:
   • Read through source 2.
   • Look for words and phrases which give a
     source 1. *Highlight them in italic.*
   Find any words or phrases which agree with the r

3. Now use the framework below to help you sum

   The views of historians about the Vikings seem to
   in 1965 had a very negative view of the Vikings. H
            **[Choose the three worst things you |
            here]**

Fig 3.1 a   continued

CD-ROM Ch3/Vikings Word doc

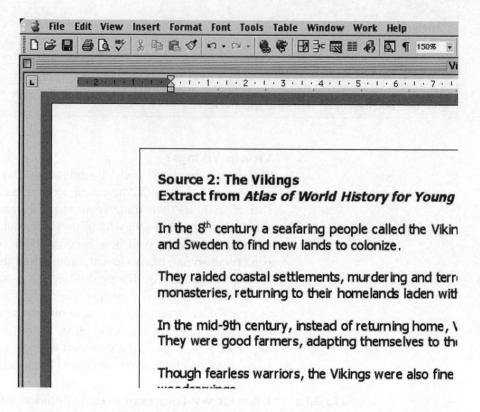

Source 2: The Vikings
Extract from *Atlas of World History for Young*

In the 8ᵗʰ century a seafaring people called the Vikin
and Sweden to find new lands to colonize.

They raided coastal settlements, murdering and terr
monasteries, returning to their homelands laden with

In the mid-9th century, instead of returning home, \
They were good farmers, adapting themselves to the

Though fearless warriors, the Vikings were also fine

As always, the key factor is not what the technology is or does but how the technology helps with learning. The example in figure 3.1a has solid credentials in terms of history and indeed a wider educational picture, and as a resource is:

➡ **Very easy to create and use.** To create this type of task, it is a simple question of copying and pasting the required section from the website. From this point only the most basic word-processing skill is needed. If you are an advanced user of ICT, then this task may be one which your less experienced colleagues would feel happier using.

➡ **Useable with a suite of computers and a whiteboard.** This is an important reminder that whatever the technology involved, the role of the teacher is still vital in terms of making sure students understand the task, finding time for feedback and discussion and generally managing the learning of the students.

➡ **An introduction to the vexed question of historical interpretation.** It is encouraging for students, however young, to read contrasting accounts of historical events and to see that the past is rarely, if ever, one story. In this exercise, students are considering how accounts of the past have changed between 1965 and 1997.

➡ **An accessible exercise.** Task 1 provides some helpful points. Differentiation could be achieved by asking some students to complete only task 1 or only tasks 1–2. Some or all of the tasks could be completed as a whole class rather than in pairs. Task 3 could be left altogether, broken down for different students to tackle different sections or tackled together as a whole class in a teacher led discussion.

➡ **An exercise with huge potential**. The task holds great potential to develop other aspects of learning alongside knowledge and understanding in history.

➡ In terms of literacy, students are dealing with texts which are often assumed to be informative texts but are in reality persuasive texts. The writing tasks require them to create persuasive texts and balanced arguments.

➡ Tasks like this could be used to help bridge the perennial problem of the KS2–3 gap. If students are familiar with a task like this on the Vikings, then it ought to be easier to ask them in KS3 to tackle the same basic exercise but on a different theme, such as the rise of Islam or the death of Thomas Becket. The potential exists here to really build progression. Students who have thought about *how* historians' views change at KS2 might be more ready to move on in KS3 to consider *why* historians' views change.

➡ It is a useful introduction to some of the functions of the word processor.

Most of the above points could legitimately be applied to this task whether it was tackled using a word processor or as a paper exercise, so a perfectly reasonable question is 'why use a word processor?' After all, tasks 1 and 2 could easily be carried out with paper copies of the sources and highlighter pens or simply underlining sections.

There are lots of good reasons for using a word processor, not least its contribution to the development of word-processing skills. However, in this instance the main role of the word processor is in building confidence. Alistair Smith and a good few other writers have pointed out how important it is to create a supportive learning environment for students. He uses the extremely useful phrase 'high challenge low threat' to help us evaluate how our students might feel about a task. This is where the word processor immediately scores over paper methods. To begin with, there is the neatness and precision with which relevant text is selected – a word processor document always looks great. This is enhanced further by the fact that if a student accidentally highlights something using a word processor, it can be undone. Better still, they might change the selected text having discussed it with a partner. This flexibility can be a big boost to self-confidence. The fact that you can undo and retry as often as you like can encourage some students to try when otherwise the threat of getting it wrong may lead them to opt out. Add a whiteboard into this heady mix and this challenging intellectual exercise becomes a little less daunting and may even become fun. The final task is still really a reading exercise, although it does involve students in some writing and editing. In fact, the teacher could easily put greater emphasis on this task, asking students to create balanced arguments from the writing framework. The teacher could even ask students to consult other sources and add points from these sources into the framework. The word processor is not essential in this exercise, but it is not hard to see how it can play a very useful role.

Women and the Great War
It is not hard to see how this role can be extended as students progress through KS3 and beyond. In figure 3.1b the task is again related to interpretations. In this instance students are asked to put themselves in the position of historians who have a fixed view on a given topic and consider how each historian would

interpret evidence so that it fitted with his/her particular view. This is an important element of understanding historical interpretations – that sometimes the way the historian 'reads' apparently objective sources are coloured by factors such as his/her pre-existing views, cultural influences, political perspectives, gender and so on. This exercise is extremely challenging in terms of getting students to effectively empathize with the historian. It requires careful thought as to how the same sources can be employed as evidence to support different interpretations of historical events. Students need to see how this is achieved, not least because the selective use and interpretation of images and source material is a feature of their everyday lives in media sources from newspapers to the internet.

Fig 3.1b   **Women and the First World War**

CD-ROM Ch3/Women WWI Word doc

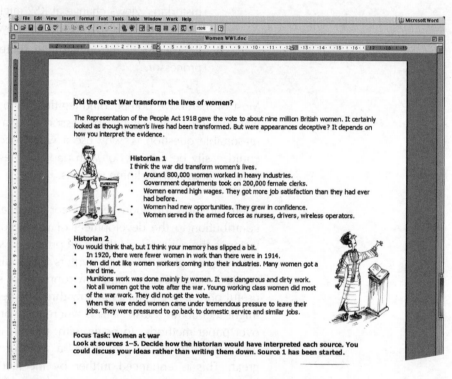

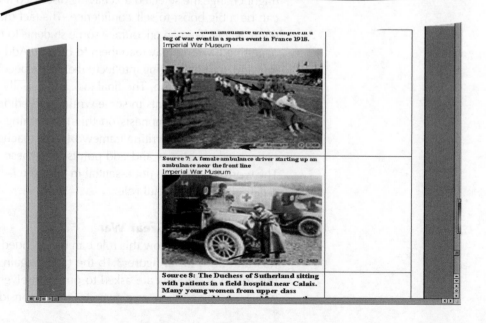

The same questions which have already been raised about why to use a word processor apply in this exercise and the responses are much the same. To begin with, it is high challenge and relatively low threat. The challenge of this exercise makes the ability of the word processor to correct and redraft especially valuable. The cells on either side of the source are small enough not to be intimidating to students who fear they will not be able to write enough, but they will grow as students write more.

It also has much to recommend it from the VAK perspective, meeting the range of learning styles of your students. The exercise can be adapted to suit students who are more visually literate by requiring a greater focus on the visual sources. Less confident students can be asked to look at a limited number of sources, or only visual sources if that is where their strengths lie. More confident students might be asked to visit websites and extend this task by selecting new sources to add to the resource and analysing them. The text in each column could be copied into another word processor document and put together to form a paragraph summarizing the views of historian 1 and those of historian 2. In a challenging task such as this, the support and range of options made available by the word processor could really help the teacher support students with a wide range of abilities.

The word processor and source analysis

The basic principles of a task such as figures 3.1a and 3.1b are easily transferable to other contexts. The most obvious is the national curriculum requirement at KS2 and KS3 that students should be able to use a range of sources in an historical enquiry and that they should be aware that sources can be problematic, depending on their nature, provenance and their relevance to a particular line of enquiry.

Nat. Curr. Ofsted

Historical enquiry
4. Pupils should be taught:
    a) how to find out about the events, people and changes studied from an appropriate range of sources of information, including ICT-based sources.

History national curriculum KS2

Nat. Curr. Ofsted

Historical enquiry
4. Pupils should be taught to:

    a) identify, select and use a range of appropriate sources of information including oral accounts, documents, printed sources, the media, artefacts, pictures, photographs, music, museums, buildings and sites, and ICT-based sources as a basis for independent historical enquiries

    b) evaluate the sources used, select and record information relevant to the enquiry and reach conclusions.

History national curriculum KS3

The Liverpool to Manchester Railway

Figure 3.2 shows an example of a primary source and a task designed to help students to analyse it. As with figures 3.1a and 3.1b, it could be tackled as a paper source, but again the word processor adds another dimension. The tasks the students are asked to tackle allow the different VAK learning styles to be applied to what is essentially a text based task. Adding headings and skimming the text to decide where headings should go helps the visual learner to create a visual map of the text. The auditory learner might well read the text to himself or herself. If you want to go technology crazy you could even use a text to speech application, such as ReadPlease (http://www.readplease.com/). The task offers less to a kinesthetic learner, although for some kinesthetic learners the motor control of the mouse does seem to help embed learning.

The word processor in this instance offers the familiar advantages over pen and paper. There are the same advantages of being able to try and retry. Task 1 of the Railway source (found on the CD-ROM), in which students have to apply headings, is a good example. The point of the task is, of course, to get students to read the source carefully and internalize its thrust and meaning. The word processor is very forgiving in a task such as this. If students put the heading on the wrong paragraph they can easily correct it. Similarly, in task 2 the word processor is very forgiving of errors. It is also, with appropriate guidance, a useful tool for getting students to examine the rhetorical devices used in the source to sell the idea of the railroad to the general public. The prospectus was not only trying to raise money. It was also trying to create a political will to get Parliament to pass legislation that would overcome the resistance of landowners opposing the proposal of railways passing through their land. This is a further dimension which the word processor can offer. This source is clearly one sided. Having tackled tasks 1 and 2, students could be asked to edit this piece and re-present it as a newspaper article giving a more even-handed analysis. For example, the article may accept the value of transporting eggs or meat quickly, but might argue that the rapid transit of boatloads of coal or iron ore is much less significant. Another argument could be that railways, regardless of quicker journey times, would still face a risk from thieves.

WEBSITE

Fig 3.2　　**Simple source based exercise using the word processor**

CD–ROM Ch3/Railway Source
Word doc

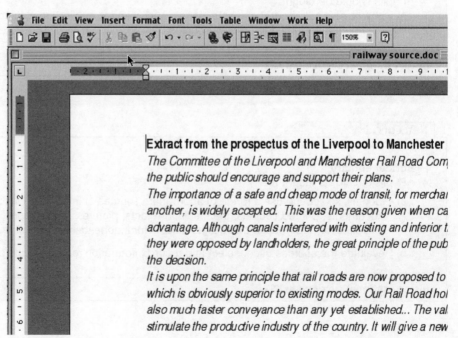

Using the word processor to help build analytical thinking and writing

It is sometimes a truism that when using the word processor in the history classroom, the simplicity of the use of technology masks the sophistication of the learning and support which is taking place. I have used the examples in figures 3.3a–c many times with students and with teachers on INSET courses and this is an issue that often emerges in discussion.

Fig 3.3a   Using the word processor for categorizing and sorting

CD-ROM Ch3/William and William Word doc

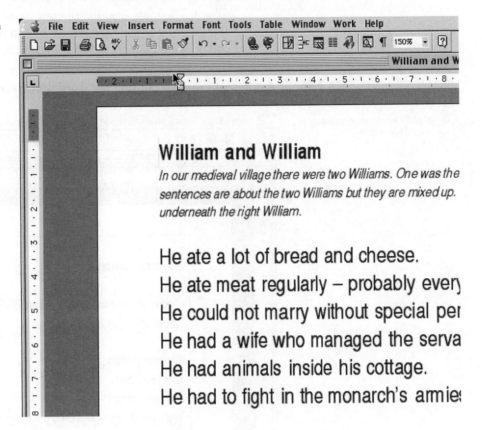

The emphasis of this exercise is on the sorting and categorizing of different pieces of historical information. Figures 3.3a–c ask students to consider the differences within an historical situation. It is most likely to be used in Year 7 as part of a unit on Medieval Britain. It could be used as an informal test at the end of a unit on life in a medieval village. Like the other examples, it is easy to replicate wherever students are required to consider different features of an historical topic.

➡ The same principle could easily be applied to a KS2 unit on the Victorians using, say, a servant and his/her employer in a big Victorian house. At KS1 it could be used to compare seaside holidays then and now (see figure 3.3b). It might just as easily apply at GCSE or AS level in an exercise comparing a supporter and opponent of prohibition in the 1920s in the USA.

➡ The task could just as easily be applied to looking at differences across periods. An exercise with that focus might contrast statements about a Roman and an Anglo-Saxon or an eighteenth-century farm worker compared to a nineteenth-century factory worker.

➡ The task could also be used to look at concepts. The list could be causes and consequences of the Russian Revolution or statements that are supported/unsupported by the available evidence on a particular issue. You could also make a list of events, personalities or developments which students then have to sort into the correct chronological periods.

➡ The task could also be used to directly target word-processing skills. With a little extra direction, students could be asked to use specific functions for specific aspects of the task. Thus, they might use 'drag and drop' for one William, while practising 'Cut and Paste' for the other William. There are also the options to introduce students to 'Copy and Paste', the use of the right mouse button menu, the 'Edit' menu and the buttons in the toolbars of the word processor.

Fig 3.3b   **A different example of using the word processor for categorizing and sorting**

CD-ROM Ch3/Seaside Holidays
Word doc

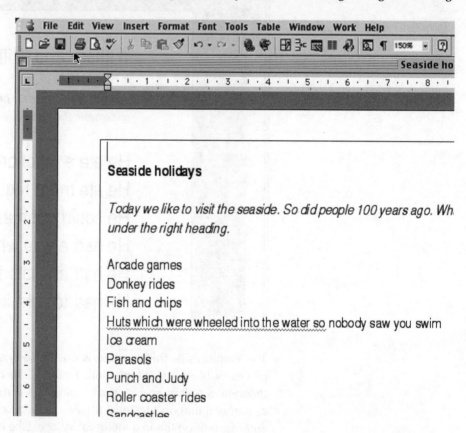

Another feature of this task is that it highlights the central role of the teacher and the management of the class. To begin with, it is just as suited as the previous examples to use with a whiteboard. However, the full value of this task is probably to be found with students working in twos or threes around a computer. In a typical class, the weaker students might require a whole lesson to complete it. Brighter students will work through the task fairly quickly and will be ready for further challenges. Managing this situation is not the remit of the technology. Whether using technology or not, the management of an educational issue, such as effective differentiation, is primarily the role of the teacher and the teacher's effective intervention in the lesson. Figure 3.3c indicates how such intervention might develop.

Fig 3.3c   Refining the task and students' writing skills

Stage 1 After the initial stage of sorting, students will have a block of information on William the lord which looks like this.	**William the lord** He ate meat regularly – probably every day He had a wife who managed the servants He had to fight in the monarch's armies, or send men to fight in his place He had to pay taxes to the monarch He lived in a large house with several rooms He owned a lot of land but did not work it He ran the local court and sorted out disputes between his tenants He was better off than a freeman His teeth were in better condition than many people's teeth today
Stage 2 At this point the teacher could ask some students to make observations about William's life compared to the other William. The word processor makes it easy for students to add their observations (shown here shaded in grey) to the text.	**William the lord had a better life than William the villein.** He ate meat regularly – probably every day He had a wife who managed the servants He had to fight in the monarch's armies, or send men to fight in his place He had to pay taxes to the monarch He lived in a large house with several rooms He owned a lot of land but did not work it He ran the local court and sorted out disputes between his tenants He was better off than a freeman His teeth were in better condition than many people's teeth today
Stage 3 At this point the demanding teacher now starts to point out that we need devices which connect the assertion with the supporting evidence. The word processor makes it easy to add these devices.	**William the lord had a better life than William the villein**. For example, he ate meat regularly – probably every day. He also had a wife who managed the servants. He had to fight in the monarch's armies, or send men to fight in his place He had to pay taxes to the monarch He lived in a large house with several rooms He owned a lot of land but did not work it He ran the local court and sorted out disputes between his tenants He was better off than a freeman His teeth were in better condition than many people's teeth today
Stage 4 Now the teacher points out that the information about William the lord contains responsibilities as well as benefits. The word processor makes it easy to reorganize this text to provide a more balanced assessment of William the lord's life.	**William the lord had a better life than William the villein**. For example, he ate meat regularly – probably every day. He also had a wife who managed the servants. He lived in a large house with several rooms whereas William the villein had one room. He owned a lot of land but did not work it. He was better off than a freeman. Finally, his teeth were in better condition than many people's teeth today. **On the other hand, William the lord did have important responsibilities**. For example, he had to fight in the monarch's armies, or send men to fight in his place. He also had to pay taxes to the monarch. In addition to this, he ran the local court and sorted out disputes between his tenants.
Stage 5 The teacher finally wants the student to cut out the extra material which does not really help the argument. The word processor's word count tool reveals that there are 127 words in this section. The teacher sets a target of getting the whole story under 100 words (also to be checked with the word count tool).	**William the lord had a better life than William the villein**. For example, he ate meat regularly – probably every day. He also had a wife who managed the servants. He owned a lot of land but did not work it like William the villein. On the other hand, William the lord did have important responsibilities. For example, he had to fight in the monarch's armies, or send men to fight in his place. In addition to this, he ran the local court and sorted out disputes between his tenants.

▌The word processor as a tool for review, revision and planning

The task involving William and William begins to get to the heart of one of the key challenges facing all teachers of history – that of getting students to communicate their ideas succinctly and effectively. This is very demanding. Writing effectively is not a process, but a series of processes. In 1998, I set out a list of these processes and pointed out why a typical student, called Gerry, finds them challenging. In short, Gerry has to …

1. Read and locate information from a source or sources of information. (*Always a challenge with Gerry.*)

2. Select information relevant to a specific purpose. (*Gerry is quite good at this.*)

3. Discard irrelevant information. (*Gerry is terrible here. It is a very threatening process when you have low self-esteem and are not prepared to trust your own judgement.*)

4. Categorize that information. (*Usually causes or consequences – Gerry is now beginning to struggle.*)

5. Refine that categorization process with factors such as religious causes or economic consequences. (*Gerry's weak short-term memory means he is now at the point where he gets lost very easily. He needs a series of hooks or pegs upon which to hang important details.*)

6. Reach judgements about the relative importance of these categories and sub-categories. (*Without support, Gerry starts drifting back into narrative because he can handle that form of writing.*)

7. Consider the inter-relationships between these categories and sub-categories. (*Gerry is now in need of counselling.*)

8. Work out a logical sequence in which to present these judgements. (*Oh yes, and the evidence that supports them...*)

9. Communicate the ideas generated in logical sequence and flowing prose. (*Gerry is rapidly losing the will to live.*)

Students all too easily fall into the trap of thinking that writing a lot of information down constitutes an effective answer to an historical question. One of the biggest factors that leads to underperformance at GCSE is students running out of time because they write too much which is not of direct relevance to the question. The discipline required in stage 5 in figure 3.3c is as relevant to students at KS2 as it is to students taking the A2 examinations.

The USA and the Vietnam War

Figures 3.4a and 3.4b demonstrates this principle in the context of students looking at the Vietnam War as part of a GCSE course. This example, and figure 3.5, owe much to the pioneering work of Terry Haydn at UEA Norwich in experimenting with the ways in which the word processor could help students manipulate text and meaning. These ideas were a guiding force behind the original history and IT Support Project materials published by NCET (National Council for Educational Technology, now renamed BECTA) and the Historical Association.

In this particular instance, students are required to work not with short sentences or bullet points but with a whole text. All of the same caveats apply to this activity as to the others mentioned in this section. The effectiveness of the activity will depend partly on the technology. It will depend much more on the teacher making sure the students are thoroughly prepared to tackle the task.

It will also depend on effective teacher intervention with the learning of individuals or groups, and also the teacher's management of the whole group. This means regular 'calling in' of the group for mini plenaries in which ideas are shared or question and answer sessions in which learning is reinforced and potential trouble spots anticipated.

Fig 3.4a Recording table for an activity designed to help students at GCSE level to locate and categorize information on the Vietnam War

CD-ROM Ch3/Vietnam War
Word doc

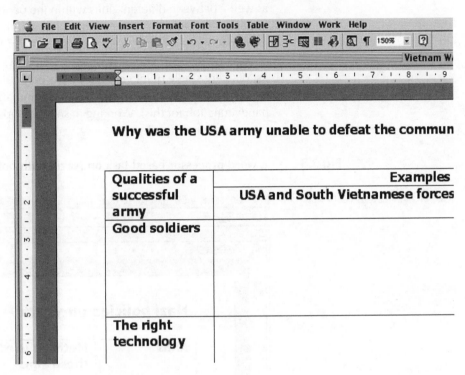

Fig 3.4b Extracts from the text used by the students as the source of information for the recording sheet.

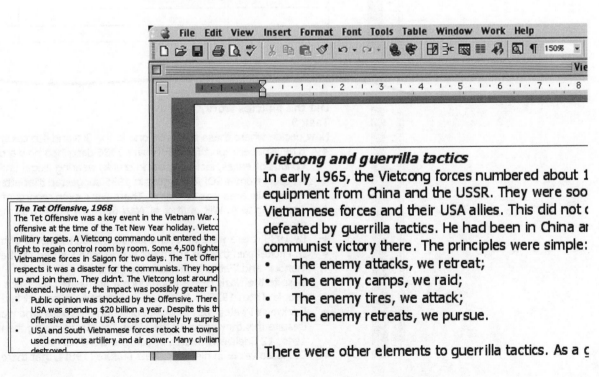

Nazi youth policies, 1933–39

Figure 3.5 shows an example designed to help students at AS level work to overcome the problem of content overload and develop an effective analytical approach. It is a good example of how the word processor can help students to connect their learning to the wider context of their work, in this case, exam preparation. We generally tend to think of connecting the learning as something which takes place at the start of a unit of study, and so it is. However, at the end of an examination course there are lots of connections to be made as well – between different units within the period of historical study and, more importantly, between the content of the unit and the requirements of the examination. In this example, the task came at the end of a unit on the impact of Nazi policies on young people in Germany, 1933–39. The teacher wrote a list of every single point covered in this particular unit. These points were then randomly jumbled (the 'Table – Sort' command of the word processor is a handy function for this). Working in small groups, students had to put the points into some kind of order.

Fig 3.5   A word processor based task on Nazi youth policies, 1933–39

CD-ROM Ch3/Nazi Youth Word doc

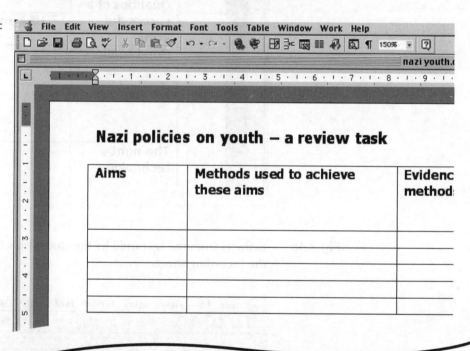

File Edit View Insert Format Font Tools Table Window Work Help

nazi youth.

Nazi policies on youth – a review task

Aims	Methods used to achieve these aims	Evidenc method:

Did the policies work?
Task 5
Now decide where these points belong in the 3rd and 4th columns.
- A newspaper report from February 1936 described how around 80 various offences, including being drunk, wearing illegal uniforms ar
- A report from a SOPADE agent in 1935 suggested that attendance Westphalia area was declining. There were even reports of Hitler Y
- According to A. Wilt, author of *Nazi Germany* (1994), as many as S regime.
- By 1939, there were an estimated six million members of the Hitle
- D. Peukel said that he and most young men learned to obey order 'honour' and 'Fatherland' were mentioned.
- Despite the Nazis desire to produce a fit master race there was no people. From 1933 to 1937 cases of diphtheria, scarlet fever and in
- Edelweiss Pirates were a loose collection of groups who were mair Despite this they opposed the Hitler Youth and during the war wer 1944, 12 Edelweiss Pirates in Cologne were hanged.
- G. Mosse wrote in his book, *Nazi Culture* (1981), that there were h

In this case, the information was sorted by column headings. It helped students to decide which points would be most appropriate to explain and or exemplify the key themes of the unit (Nazi aims, methods, evidence of success, evidence of lack of success). This was a helpful review task. It also generated some interesting discussion because, in the nature of history, many of the points could have been allocated in more than one area. In particular, many of the policies that belonged in the column on methods could legitimately be seen as methods which tried to achieve more than one aim.

So far so good. Using the word processor made the sorting, trying out and correcting easy and painless. Points could even be copied and pasted into two categories if this was felt to be necessary. The students were happy and secure in their knowledge and understanding. None of the bullet points were unfamiliar. The material felt less overwhelming because they had to some extent tamed it by categorizing and sorting it. They also had a great big resource packed with information which they could use in their revision. There was a strong sense that they now 'knew' this topic.

This of course was the ideal point to upset the apple cart. A bit of thought led the students to realize that the completed table contained far more material here than could be used in an answer to an examination question to be answered in about 35 minutes. There was nothing for it – they would have to cut out roughly two-thirds of the material in the table if they were going to leave themselves with a plan for an essay that could realistically be written in 35 minutes. Here again the word processor helped. The completed table was saved and students edited down a copy. They were able to cut sections and then see how this affected the overall balance of the material. After much heartache, they were able to 'ditch' a lot of material and emerge with a plan for an essay that would be manageable in the time allocated.

The word processor: Review and preview

The activities outlined in this chapter of the book are all concerned with work using text – a staple of the history classroom. One of the concerns which many teachers feel is that they do not have time to create such resources. This is perhaps less of a worry than it should be. To begin with, typing out a block of text does not always take as long as we fear. More importantly, there are many websites that can be used as quarries of source material for exercises like the ones in this section. The Internet History Sourcebooks Project is an excellent source of primary source text material (http://www.fordham.edu/halsall/). Secondary sources and also novels can be found in electronic form at Project Gutenberg (http://promo.net/pg/history.html). The fact that these sources are already in electronic form greatly reduces the preparation time. There are plenty of other sources such as CD-ROM encyclopedias as well.

WEBSITE

WEBSITE

Another new development should also help teachers to use these types of activities with relatively limited preparation time. Several publishers are now developing CD-ROM materials to accompany their textbooks, aiming primarily to help teachers exploit the full potential of whiteboard technology (see chapter 2, pages 35–36). The example on page 56 comes from *GCSE Modern World History* published by Hodder Murray. Clearly, access to the text of the main textbook used in the history lessons opens up exciting possibilities to blur the traditional boundary between textbook and technology.

Fig 3.6 An example of the new generation of CD-ROM resources designed to support textbooks. In this example, a section of text has been selected and appears in a new window. It can be highlighted and/or opened separately in a word processor file for further editing, analysis or manipulation

CD–ROM Ch3/Hodder Murray/GCSE_MWH_Demo

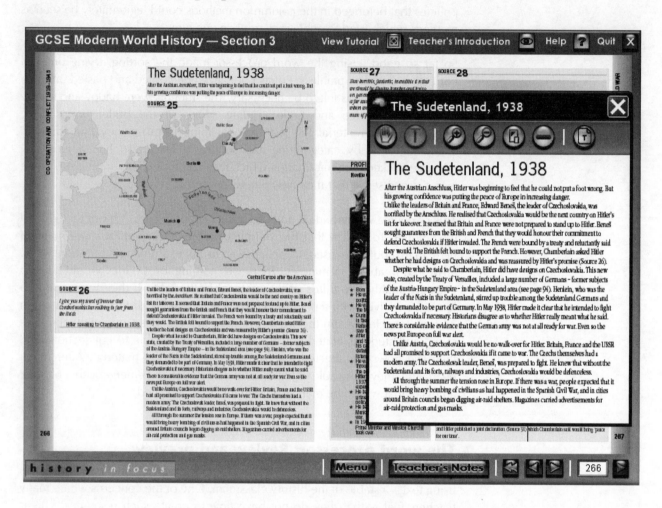

Screen shot of 'The Sudenland, 1938' from the CD-ROM *GCSE Modern World History, Electronic Edition,* Hodder Murray (yet to be published), reproduced by permission of Hodder Murray.

Chapter 4

Dynamic data handling

In this section you will discover:

- History has large amounts of excellent source material which is extremely well suited to manipulation in data handling software.
- Data handling software presents exciting opportunities to cater for the preferred learning style of the mathematical logical learner in history based enquiries.
- Learning objectives in history and ICT complement each other particularly well in the area of data handling.
- Data files can be extremely useful in helping students to gain overviews of periods. Data files can also help students understand past societies at a detailed and complex level.
- Data handling provides opportunities for students to visualize complex concepts.
- Data handling can be humorous and fun!
- Data can come in many different forms and is generally most powerful when used in tandem with other source material.
- Data handling work in history can have powerful resonance in citizenship, ICT and vocational dimensions of the curriculum.

▌Data and the history teacher

We tend to think of history as a literary subject, and for the most part it is. That said it would be a great disservice to the subject to ignore some of the potential for use of data and data handling software in history. There are many good reasons for trying to find a more prominent role for data handling. To begin with, history has such wonderful sources of fascinating data, possibly more than any other subject. History has census data – plentiful records from Britain's schools, hospitals and prisons. The armed forces have long collected data on recruitment and casualties. The Great War generated countless memorials which are a potential source of data. All of these sources of information provide an insight into the lives of people, and sometimes whole populations, in the past. Large data sources can often complement more localized, personal sources in a sophisticated enquiry, which challenges students to show high levels of critical thinking and initiative. Another critical point is that whereas many of the tasks performed by the word processor in the previous chapter could have been carried out using pen and paper, this is not the case with data handling. The speed and flexibility of data handling software in searching, sorting and graphing data simply cannot be matched by other means.

There is also great potential for history and ICT to complement each other very strongly in the area of data handling. One problem for many ICT co-ordinators is getting hold of data files, especially large data files. History is blessed in this area. History also has a methodology of investigation and creative thinking which lends itself to the effective exploitation of the power of data handling software. For example, at KS2 and KS3 the national curriculum history orders require that students should be taught about 'the characteristic features of the periods studied'. They also require that students learn about 'social, cultural, religious and ethnic diversity of the societies studied'. There are many ways in which teachers can and do tackle these challenging requirements. The aim here is not to say that they *should* be taught using data files, but simply that these and numerous other aspects of history *can* be taught using data files.

Big pictures and little pictures

Ofsted and other research reports have shown that many students enjoy studying the individual elements that make up an historical enquiry but they sometimes struggle to piece this together into a bigger picture of the features of a society being studied. Many teachers have experimented with the possibility that a small-scale study can throw light on a bigger picture but not often through the use of data handling. It's a pity data handling has not been more widely used as it's a tool that can help us to help students to access the bigger picture of an historical period. Activities that use data handling also create opportunities for a VAK friendly approach. In the examples below, we explore how difficult concepts like the multifaceted nature of a past society can be made more accessible by representing them as visual images. The nature of data handling also tends to highlight the actual learning processes very powerfully – arguably more powerfully than in any other type of ICT-based work. The nature of data handling requires us to consider the nature of the data we have, what we are able to do with it and whether it really supports the claims we are making from it. British Prime Minister Benjamin Disraeli famously spoke of 'Lies, damned lies and statistics'. In a recent updating of this statement, a government statistician admitted in a radio interview that 'if you torture the data enough it will eventually tell you what you want to hear'.

Victorian Homes

Figure 4.1 shows sections from the National Archives Learning Curve Snapshot resource on Victorian Homes. The task uses a very small sample of a data rich source – a census record – alongside street maps and photographs. The aim is for students to examine the differences in affluence between two households relatively near to each other. In doing so, students begin to see how data such as this is used by historians. They also see how this small-scale use of data provides a small-scale snapshot of the bigger picture of divisions in Victorian society.

Fig 4.1   Extracts from the Victorian Homes resource on the National Archives Learning Curve website

WEBSITE   http://www.learningcurve.gov.uk/snapshots/snapshot14/snapshot14.htm

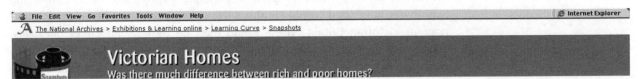

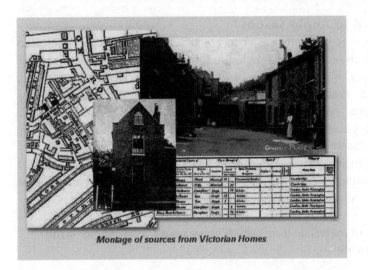

Montage of sources from Victorian Homes

This opening montage indicates the ways in which the resource brings home to students that the best way to try and reconstruct the lives of people in the past is usually from a range of sources. In this instance, street maps, photographs of actual houses and their specific census records from 1891 come together to give us a vivid picture of the contrasts between two households in Victorian Britain.

3. Now view the census return for some houses in Conduit Place to find out more.

3a. What type of work did the head of the household do?

3b. Did the children go out to work?

3c. Did the wives go out to work?

3d. Who other than the Harding family lived at 5 Conduit Place?

3e. What else do you notice about the Harding family?

3f. Why do you think they had a lodger living with them?

3g. Conduit Place does not exist today. Make a list of reasons why it might have been demolished.

Source 3: Census Return for numbers 5, 6, and 7 Conduit Place

It is the students, with some careful guidance, who create this picture. Here are a series of structured questions about the working class house in Conduit Place. The questions are mostly closed, factual questions, but they are phrased in such a way as to lead students towards a realization of how apparently dry data, such as this, can actually help reconstruct past lives.

5. Now view a census return for a house in Clapton Road.

5a. What does James Bourklebank do for a living?

5b. How many children does he have?

5c. Is this family middle class or working class?

Source 5: Census Return for Vine Cottage, Clapton Road (1881)

6. Create a list of: similarities between the rich and poor families : differences between the rich and poor families.

7. If your house is over 100 years contact your local archive to find the census records and see who lived there.

The middle class house on Clapton Road is given the same treatment. The final questions encourage students to make comparisons between the two houses and do some investigating of their own.

Figure 4.1 may not be exactly what a purist would call a data handling activity, but it is an engaging task using data sources. It also gives students a good platform for understanding how data can be used, and how even a small data set can at the very least be used to generate hypotheses. In this case, the hypotheses generated would be about the extent of contrast between rich and poor in Victorian Britain. These could then be tested with larger data sets, and/or with the use of other sources. This approach of using a small data set to generate hypotheses is applicable to many other historical topics and themes. Two such examples can be seen below in figures 4.3a and 4.3b.

What mattered to Anglo-Saxons?

Not surprisingly, it is generally easier to create and use data files relating to more recent periods of history, thanks to the survival of records from these latter periods. Figure 4.2, however, shows us that there are exceptions to this rule. This data file was downloaded from a website on Anglo-Saxon archaeology

WEBSITE (http://mscitprojects.arts.gla.ac.uk/9344501m/Anglo/Download_files/index.asp). It was chosen because it contained information that focused on day-to-day aspects of Anglo-Saxon lives. It was also chosen because it offered a relatively rare opportunity in which the student who has a strong preference for logical mathematical learning would be able to work in their preferred learning style in the course of an historical investigation.

Fig 4.2   **The distribution of materials from which grave goods in an Anglo-Saxon cemetery were made**

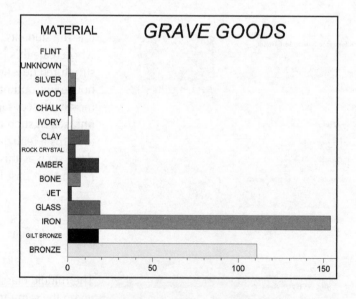

CD–ROM Ch4/Abingdon grave goods data file

This graph was drawn using data downloaded from the website, which was then put into a data handling package and simplified by deleting some of the original files. By removing some of the fields in the data file, it becomes a usable source for primary school students looking at the question of what mattered to Anglo-Saxons. The first stage of such an exercise could be to ask students to imagine that a dear friend is moving to live in another country. If students were Anglo-Saxons, they would show how much this person meant to them by giving them something they valued. It seems likely that toys, electronic goods, clothing and footballs might all be on the list. Taking this as their preparation, students could then see what goods Anglo-Saxons gave to their friends and family as they journeyed into the after life. The database software would allow students to search and graph the most common artefacts and also what these artefacts were made of. They could then be asked to hypothesize about such issues as:

➡ the materials and technology available to the Anglo-Saxons

➡ what the goods suggested about Anglo-Saxon daily lives

➡ what they suggested about Anglo-Saxon religious beliefs.

These hypotheses might then be tested against a wider range of text and other sources.

Domesday Dorset

Figure 4.3a and 4.3b show pie charts drawn from the data of a small data file drawn up from the Domesday Book for Dorset in 1087. One of the great assets of data handling software is its ability to make graphic representations of concepts such as change over time. Many students find such concepts difficult to grasp, but in this example the pattern emerging for Dorset seems very clear. The majority of students would be able to hypothesize from this result that if the Dorset pattern were replicated then the Saxon landholding class was effectively wiped out after the Norman Conquest. These pie charts were drawn with a relatively simple data file of just 30 records. That said, the structure of the data file was carefully thought out so that the data entered could be interrogated meaningfully by students (see pages 63–64 on creating and using data files). This was one of many data files originally developed by Dave Martin of the Dorset LEA and which became the backbone of the pioneering BECTA/Historical Association publications on the use of data handling in history.

Fig 4.3a   **Ownership of land in Dorset before the Norman Conquest in 1066**

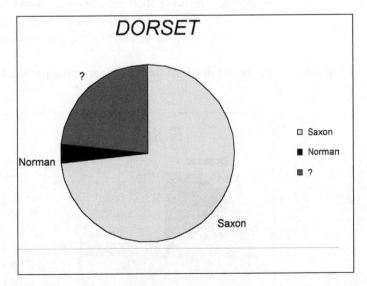

(? = No record of owner)

Fig 4.3b   Ownership of land in Dorset in 1087

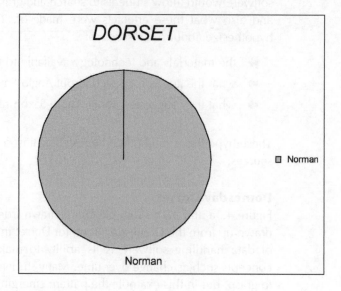

Britain 1500–1750

CD−ROM Ch4/Britain 1500–1750 data file

Figures 4.4a and 4.4b used a small data file of just 14 records. These records were the monarchs who ruled Britain in the period 1500–1750. Students were asked to consider whether the data suggested that the period was a stable one or one riddled with upheaval. Here they were challenged to look at the data available and to consider what data and what patterns would provide meaningful answers. The data file offered a range of possibilities. Figure 4.4a and 4.4b show that in this case it was quite possible to find contrasting messages emerging from the available evidence. This was a valuable lesson for the students, and a timely reminder that history is a complex subject that often throws up sources which conflict, making it difficult to interpret and use as evidence. The idea that the past is a complex world full of contrasts and contradictions is, surprisingly, an idea which many students struggle to grasp even though they recognize that the present is complex and contradictory.

Fig 4.4a   **Causes of death of British rulers in the period 1500–1750**

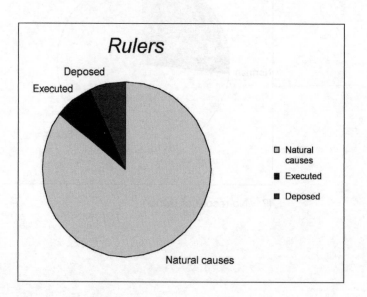

Fig 4.4b   **The relationship between the outgoing and incoming monarchs in the period 1500–1750**

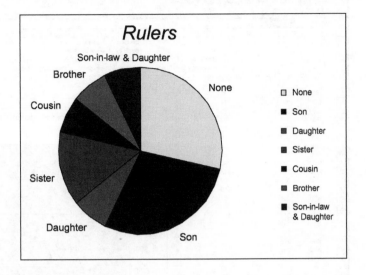

These two pie charts again show the value of the ability of data handling software to make difficult concepts into visual images. In figure 4.4a, the pie chart suggests that Britain was a stable place. In contrast, figure 4.4b suggests a different picture. In the sixteenth and seventeenth centuries a trouble free succession would usually be one from father to son. This is clearly not the case in the majority of successions.

Together, the two pie charts suggest a period in which there is stability and turbulence. Students now have a broad hypothesis to be tested using other elements of the data in the data file and of course more detailed case studies of particular reigns. Whatever the next step, the ability of the data handling software here is important. It effectively translates the difficult idea that Britain was neither wholly stable nor wholly in turmoil into visual images.

▌ Creating and using data files

In general terms, there are two main types of data files that can be used in the history classroom. One is a digital version of an original data source such as a census. We will look at these a little later. The other type of data file is the file created by a teacher and/or his students to help them carry out a particular investigation. When creating a data file there are two main considerations:

➡ The data handling software to be used: There are two main types of data handling software – the spreadsheet and the database.

➡ The structure of the data file to be created: This is critical to making the use of data handling software a meaningful experience for students.

The spreadsheet

In a spreadsheet the data is organized in columns and rows. From the historian's point of view, it is typically most useful when examining data files which are mostly numerical. Figure 4.5 shows a small extract from a very large spreadsheet file showing trends in crime in the United Kingdom in the twentieth century. Teachers can access a wide range of statistical sources from the Home Office (http://www.homeoffice.gov.uk) and the Office for National Statistics (www.statistics.gov.uk).

WEBSITE
WEBSITE

Fig 4.5   A spreadsheet of British crime figures, 1900–2001

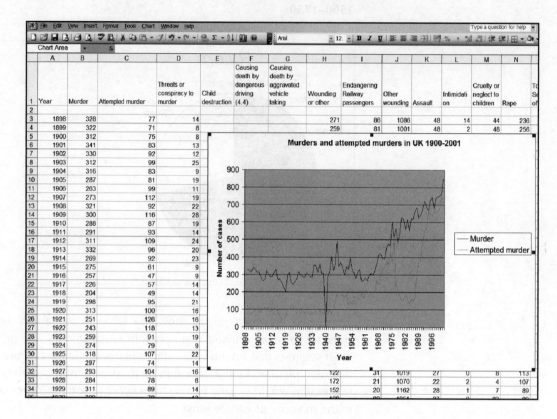

This is an example of one of the functions that the spreadsheet does very well – graphing trends in large data sets over a period of time. The spreadsheet also carries out a range of mathematical functions extremely efficiently. For example, it is relatively simple with a spreadsheet to take a section of data and ask the software to calculate average figures, or average increases in particular fields over given periods of time. Thus a spreadsheet can be used to investigate whether trade between the port of Bristol and a particular area of the empire increased or decreased at a greater or lesser rate in particular decades of the eighteenth century. The spreadsheet can also search, sort and filter data. Thus, in the data file for figure 4.5 the spreadsheet could be used to select years in which the number of incidents of assault was greater than 50. From this selected sample further searches and sorts could be carried out. This might be used to explore the current picture in a particular locality, a process made possible by another new government resource called Neighbourhood Statistics (http://neighbourhood.statistics.gov.uk/). This site allows the user to investigate crime (and a range of other figures) using recent data by postcode area.

WEBSITE

The database

The main difference between the database and spreadsheet is that in a database the data is organized in records – I find it is easier to visualize this as a stack of record cards on top of each other. Figure 4.6 shows an example of a typical database record, in this instance one of a set of nearly 400 prisoners in Huntingdon County Jail in the 1870s.

Fig 4.6   One record from the Huntingdon Jail data set published by Logotron with their database software Viewpoint. The entire data file is on the CD-ROM which accompanies this book.

CD-ROM Ch 4/Huntingdon Jail–
Prisoner Records data file

Entries in the 'Habitual Criminals' Register 1870 - 1878
HUNTINGDON COUNTY GAOL

Photograph of prisoner

Date of entry 4th Jun 1870

Year of entry 1870

Forenames Thomas

Surname Goodjohn

Aliases

Age on discharge 39

Height in feet and inches 5ft 7½in

Height in cm(approx) 170

Hair colour Light Brown

Eye colour Grey

Complexion Sallow

Where born? St Ives   *Married or Single?* Single

Trade or occupation Labourer   *Sex* male ☑ female ☐

Any other distinguishing marks? Paralysed on left side

Address at time of apprehension St Ives

Whether summarily disposed of or tried by jury Summarily

Place of conviction St Ives   *Date of conviction* 7th Mar 1870

Offence for which convicted Stealing

As a general rule, the database has more to offer the historian than the spreadsheet, although it must be stressed that this is a very general rule. Databases have a number of features which particularly suit the types of enquiries historians want to carry out. They also tend to present the results of these particular types of enquiries in a manageable and accessible way. For example, if we wanted to examine the background of male prisoners aged 30–40 then both spreadsheet and database could easily be used to select this group. At this point, however, the database would be able to draw a graph of the distribution of occupations of these men. The spreadsheet would not be able to do this without writing a macro (a mini program) which is complicated and can sometimes fall foul of virus protection software.

Software and file formats

The most common database found in schools is probably Microsoft Access. Unfortunately for historians, this software has the same graphing limitations as the spreadsheet. If history teachers want to explore data sets in the ways already suggested then they may have to discuss other software with their ICT colleagues. This may not necessarily be a problem, as one of the key elements of the ICT national curriculum is for students to become aware of the advantages and disadvantages of different software for different types of uses and audiences. Microsoft Access is an excellent storage and retrieval system, for example. If students wanted to put together an oral history archive of interviews with local people then Access would be an excellent tool for storing and managing text, photographs, video and/or sound recordings. For exploring the patterns and trends contained within a census data file you may need to look at other software such as Viewpoint by Logotron (www.logotron.co.uk/cat/view/viewpoint.html), Information Workshop by Black Cat Software (www.blackcatsoftware.com/catalog/products/infoworkshops.html) or Find It! by Actis (www.actis.co.uk/highlights/findit.html). Links to the websites of these companies can be found in section 4 on the CD-ROM which accompanies this book. Most of the data files referred to and used in this chapter are also available on the CD-ROM. They are all in one format, known as 'CSV'. This format is a basic format that can be opened or imported by virtually all data handling software.

WEBSITE

WEBSITE

The purpose of data files

Having identified the best software for the job, it is just as important to plan the record structure of the data file. The vital point here is to have a clear idea of the purpose for which the data file will be used. A good example is shown in figure 4.7, which comes from a data file of the graves in the Sheffield General Cemetery from 1836–56. The data was collected and transcribed by the Friends of the Cemetery, and has subsequently been used by students in primary and secondary schools in the surrounding area.

Fig 4.7 **A record from the database of the Friends of the Sheffield General Cemetery**

WEBSITE

http://www.gencem.org/burialrecords/records.php

(Home page is http://www.gencem.org/index.html)

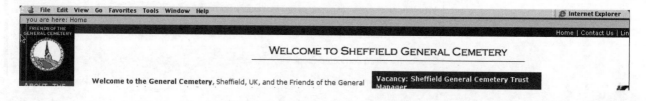

Burial	1
Year	1836
Grave	LL70
Death date	23/05/1836
Burial date	26/05/1836
First name	Mary Ann
Surname	FISH
Age	24
Description	Wife of James Fish, Bookkeeper.
Residence	Farm Bank, Shrewsbury Rd., Sheffield
Cause	Consumption
Birth	Hull, 1812
Parents	William & Ann Tummon
Parents description	Mariner & Shipowner
Informant	James Fish

The purpose of the data file was to identify patterns and developments that would help students to gain some sense of everyday life in a big Victorian city. For example, Mary Ann Fish was only 24 when she died. Was it common for people to die so young? The fact that this data file has a field which records the age of death allows the user to find out how common it was. A quick search tells us that 43 of the 5,783 graves are those of deceased aged 24. Clearly this is not terribly revealing, so we can then improve the search to look for anyone aged in their 20s. Having located these individuals, the field 'Cause' allows us to examine the different causes of death of 20 year olds. Other fields allow the user to map the deceased 20 years olds against the parts of the city they came from, the occupations of the deceased or their parents and so on. The key point is that this database was constructed with fields which would facilitate the analysis of the data contained in it. In addition, we have a resource which gives us enormous potential for a powerful multisensory investigation into the Sheffield of the early to mid Victorian period. The resources on the website contain a range of excellent ideas for making use of the site on a field visit – ideal for the kinesthetic learner. The size and scale of the data file again favours the logical mathematical learner. A range of contemporary sources on Victorian Sheffield on the internet such as Picture Sheffield

WEBSITE

(http://www.picturesheffield.com/index.html) would allow auditory and visual learners to compare and contrast the patterns in the data file with the impressions given in those contemporary sources.

It would appear that Sheffield is something of a hotbed for research using data files in history. Figure 4.8 shows the first of 50 records from a data file of cinemas in Sheffield in 1931. The data originates from an academic study by M.J. Lewis and Roger Lloyd Jones of Sheffield Hallam University. The data itself is most interesting, and could be used in an investigation such as 'Was it possible to have fun during the Depression?' What is just as interesting, however, is the clarity of purpose that underpinned the construction of the data file in the first place. For example, the 'Address' field was included in order to allow for plotting the distribution of cinemas across the city and asking whether they were more or less prominent in affluent or less affluent areas. The 'Date of opening' field allows the user to chart developments such as whether new cinemas were opening in the 1930s. Price of entry could give an indication of disposable income in a particular area of the city in 1931.

Fig 4.8 **Records from the survey of Sheffield cinemas in 1931 carried out by M.J. Lewis and Roger Lloyd Jones of Sheffield Hallam University**

CD-ROM Ch 4/Sheffield cinemas data file

	A	B	C	D	
1	Recordnumber	Cinema	Address	Financial control	
2					
3	1	Globe Picture Palace	Eccleshall Rd	Eccleshall Picture Palace Ltd	
4	2	Theatre Royal	Attercliffe	Bryan W	
5	3	Unity Picture Palace	Langsett Rd	Upperthorpe Picture Palace Co Ltd	
6	4	Norfolk Picture Palace	Duke St	Norfolk Picture House Co Ltd	
7	5	Abbeydale Picture House	Abbeydale Rd	Abbeydale Picture Co	
8	6	Electra Palace	Fitzalan Sq	Sheffield District Cinemas Ltd	
9	7	Heeley Green Picture Palace	Gleadless Rd	Heeley Green Picture House Ltd	
10	8	Page Hall Cinema	Firth Park	Page Hall Cinema Ltd	
11	9	Woodseats Picture Palace	Chesterfield Rd	Heeley & Amalgamated Cinemas Ltd	
12	10	Regent Theatre	Upwell St	Bronson J	
13	11	Picture Palace	High Green	G Woflender	
14	12	Attercliffe Pavilion	Attercliffe	Attercliffe Picture Co	
15	13	Heeley Colisium	London Rd	Heeley Colisium Ltd	
16	14	Park Picture Palace	South Road	Grosvenor Estate Co Ltd	
17	15	Kinema House	Crookes Place	Grosvenor Estate Co Ltd	
18	16	Tinsley Picture Palace	Tinsley	Wincobank Picture Co Ltd	
19	17	Woodhouse Picture Palace	Market Place	Scala Cinemas	

(Sheffield Cine...)

Sources of data and data files

In many of the examples so far, enthusiastic teachers and academics have carried out some research and typed up the results of their work into a spreadsheet or database file. This work is not as onerous as it might first appear. However, it is simply not realistic to expect classroom teachers to spend hours typing data from original sources into data handling packages on a regular basis. There are also other possible options for getting data typed up in the first instance.

➡ It might be done as part of an ICT project in which students have to create a data file. Data handling, especially handling large data files, has proved to be one of the trickier areas of teaching national curriculum ICT so it may be that history and ICT can find some common ground here.

➡ It may be possible to get students creating data files, perhaps typing 20–30 records each in a lesson and then merging these small files into one large file. Using this approach, it would take an average class one lesson to create a data file of 500–750 records.

Of course, a much more attractive option for most teachers is to make use of data files which already exist. At present there are relatively few commercially available data files. Logotron publish a collection of historical data files with their database software Viewpoint, including the excellent data file on the prisoners in Huntingdon Jail, featured later in this chapter. Another honourable exception which specializes in statistical data for education is SECOS.

WEBSITE

Teachers should not despair, however, as there are plenty of other sources of data files. The London Grid for Learning has an extensive collection of data files – available free of charge – from the 1891 census for the London Boroughs. There are also quite a lot of other census data files for different areas available from the websites of genealogy enthusiasts, although some companies do charge for their data. There are some major online data files for British history. Two of the most impressive are the National Archives 1901 census and the Commonwealth War Graves Commission website. This latter holds data on the graves of all Commonwealth servicemen and women from the Great War onwards. There is also a great deal of useful material for the study of American history. The US Census Bureau puts a good deal of its material online, and allows users to search a range of data. So too does the University of Virginia online census search. Links to all these websites can be found in chapter 4 on the CD-ROM that accompanies this book.

WEBSITES

Perhaps the line of approach which holds out the greatest potential for teachers is to try to make contact with their local higher education institution. Many academic research projects now make use of data files as part of their methodology – the Sheffield cinema data file and Anglo-Saxon graves data file being examples of this. Academic historians are usually happy to establish links with schools and help out as far as they can, so it may be that there are some interesting data files ready to use in local universities or colleges. If there is no local institution, a good place to try is the Arts and Humanities Data Service (formerly the History Data Service). This is a repository for academic data projects and is primarily aimed at Higher Education. However, schools are eligible to use the service.

WEBSITE

Enquiries and investigations with data

Of course, the point of investing time and effort into creating data files and learning how to make use of them is so that students can get their teeth into an investigation that they will find enjoyable and challenging. Here it is important to be aware of the potential which data handling offers. The control which it gives students over the nature and direction of an investigation can be exhilarating. It is especially effective when students are working collaboratively. In this instance, many heads really are better than one because, in a group, students are usually more inclined to experiment and take risks in terms of the searches performed with the data. They are also more likely when working collaboratively to devise imaginative methods of using the functionality of the software to carry out the data sort they require. It is another good example of an Alistair Smith activity which is high challenge and low threat. It is also rewarding for students. In my experience there is little which students of all ages like more than discovering facts which their teacher did not know! That said, the same control and responsibility can be daunting for students as well. As always, the solution here will come down to effective planning, preparation and intervention at appropriate moments by the teacher.

Prisoners in Huntingdon Jail, 1870–78

Figure 4.9 gives us an example of this. Here the key source of information is a database of records of prisoners in Huntingdon Jail. The task that accompanies the data file has three main aims:

➡ to provide a context for using the database software and help students develop their skills in using it

➡ to encourage critical and analytical thinking in solving the problems set by the task

➡ to encourage students to take control of the resource and take it in new directions using the functionality of the data handling software.

The opening task addresses the issue of using the software while making the activity light hearted. The task requires a degree of skill and knowledge in terms of searching the data file. Just as important, the clues become trickier as the task progresses. They begin to require a degree of lateral thinking. The task could easily be differentiated by asking students to work in pairs or groups and of course providing extra guidance on the searches to perform. However, it is important not to be too quick to provide guidance on thinking – what to search – while providing guidance on process – how to search. A good example of this may well be the reference to the female prisoners not being habitual criminals. Blunkett rather gives the game away by pointing to aliases and previous convictions. If you really wanted to stretch the critical thinking abilities of able students you could remove this additional help and simply ask them to work out whether the women were not mostly habitual criminals. It would be up to students to work out how valuable the alias and previous convictions fields are in this instance.

Task 2 takes this exercise to a higher level with some quite tricky searches and graphing tasks and some more heavy duty lateral thinking. Again, the task could be differentiated in several ways. For example, the opinions and factual statements could be underlined or even copied straight into the table for task 2. Task 3 is again designed to promote thinking, especially the extension task. Again, the task might be differentiated by asking students simply to think about one area (for example, age, sentencing and so on).

Fig 4.9   Huntingdon Jail activities

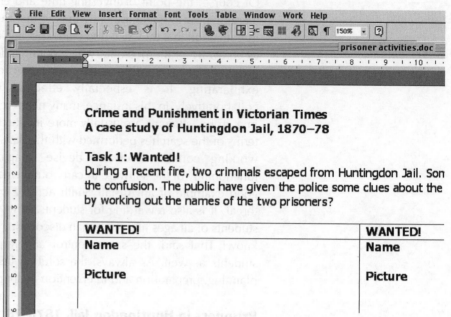

File Edit View Insert Format Font Tools Table Window Work Help

prisoner activities.doc

Crime and Punishment in Victorian Times
A case study of Huntingdon Jail, 1870–78

Task 1: Wanted!
During a recent fire, two criminals escaped from Huntingdon Jail. Son
the confusion. The public have given the police some clues about the
by working out the names of the two prisoners?

WANTED!	WANTED!
Name	Name
Picture	Picture

Task 2: Help the Home Secretary
The Home Secretary is the politician in the British government in char
them but he does not know much about them. He has sent one of his
However, Josiah Blunkett sometimes says things without fully checkin
wants you to look at Josiah's report on Huntingdon Jail and see if it fi

Read Blunkett's report first. Then complete the table which follows it.

On arriving at Huntingdon Jail, I was met by one of the senior warder
extensive tour of the jail. While I was there I was able to observe mai

As you know, I visited the jail in 1878. This was not a bad year for co
appears to have been the worst. Most of the men who have passed th
convictions – not like the women. A large number of the male prisone
shows they are a devious bunch.

my visit and was able to s--

the available data. Some are just bia.....
in it which are not supported by the facts. You can either delete t
supported by the data.

- EXTENSION TASK: There are many areas of data in the data file 1
  Add new sections to the report based on your findings from the d
  from the report if that helps. You could look at issues such as:
  o More analysis on the appearance of the prisoners – did bl
  o More analysis of the dates of convictions – could they be
  o The types of trials and sentences they received – did sun
  o Ages of the prisoners – why are there so many children?
  o Sentences – were men, women and children treated the s
  o Offences – what were the most common offences?
  o Your own investigations.
Make sure that you indicate which statements you make are facts bas
from the data.

▌ Beyond history and data handling

A template

The Huntingdon Jail task should raise a wide range of points for the history teacher beyond its obvious utilitarian value as an enjoyable task. To begin with, the basic exercise is a template that could be applied to many large data files. For example, task 1 could be used to track down two individuals in a local census file. Task 2 might be based on an account of a local area concocted by the teacher, or an extract from a local history book or website, or perhaps even an extract from a local newspaper written around the time of the census. One example was explored on pages 19–20 of chapter 1. Figure 4.10 shows an example of just such a task using data from Coalbrookdale in 1851 but which could be applied to any locality at almost any census year.

Fig 4.10   **An investigation based on census data for Coalbrookdale in 1851**

CD–ROM Ch 4/Coalbrookdale
1851 – Activity Word doc

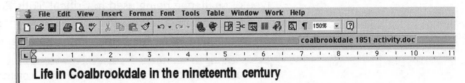

File Edit View Insert Format Font Tools Table Window Work Help

coalbrookdale 1851 activity.doc

Life in Coalbrookdale in the nineteenth century

How do we know about life in Coalbrookdale and other industrial areas in Victorian paper sources are really useful. The trouble is, they do not tell us much about ordina document which does tell us about everybody is the census. You are going to study with a little help from two guides.

Task 1: Find your guides
The point of this activity is to get familiar with how the database works. You will have the search facilities in the database.

Clues to Guide 1	How many people could it be?	Clues to Guide 2
• Guide 1 is a girl		• Guide 2 is a boy
• If you are in Year 9, she is about the same age as you		• If you are in Year 9, than you
• There are six people in her family		• There are five peopl
• She was born in Madeley, in Shropshire		• He was born in Mad
		• He works as an iron

coalbrookdale 1851 activity.doc

Task 4: Coalbrookdale according to Jane and Enoch

Jane's story
Hello! My name is Jane Bassett, and I work as a house servant in Coalbrookdale. It's a fun these census people asking everybody questions. I cannot see the point myself - everyone houses around here.

Enoch says it's got something to do with taxes, but I think he's making it up - he does that a going for him. To begin with, he has a good job. His father got him the job, just like he did boys get a better deal than the girls. Most of the girls my age, say about 14 to 16 years old, most of the boys under 16 are also still in school. At least I am not still there!

The thing is though, what have the girls got to look forward to? Most of us will end up as se

activity is to see whether you really understand how

from the database (any age, family size, occupatic

ones in activity 1

Vocational dimension

The activity is also an example of the relevance of historical methods of working to the modern world of work. The lateral thinking, teamwork (if taught that way) and use of evidence to support views are all commonplace processes in the modern world of work in the information economy. The actual processes of keying in search terms and parameters is directly related to the work of many call centre operatives in travel, insurance, banking and countless other industries where a customer information database is used. Arguably a more exciting vocational area than these is the media. Thanks to lottery funding through the New Opportunities Fund, a huge amount of the catalogue of the ITN/British Pathe archive is available online to all users free of charge. We will explore the use of video in chapter 7, but it is worth remembering that the catalogue itself is a huge database. A possible history/ICT activity using this database might be to put the students into the role of film researchers and set them an assignment such as that in figures 4.11a and 4.11b. As well as being an interesting exercise in historical interpretations, it is a good example of the type of challenge being used in Critical Skills Programmes.

Fig 4.11a   An assignment using the British Pathe catalogue

You are a researcher working for a television company. The company has produced a television series on the history of the twentieth century. They want you to put together a very short sequence of very short clips which will run at the start of each episode. Your budget is £1,800 and using the clips costs £15 per second. You might want to include clips which show themes such as:

- Warfare
- Entertainment
- Work
- Travel
- Science and technology
- Medicine and health
- The developing world
- Religion

Use the Pathe catalogue (http://www.britishpathe.com/advanced_search.php) to select your clips and then present your recommendations in this format.

Section	Theme covered	Brief description and explanation of significance of what is in this section	Pathe clip number	Length in seconds and section of clip (e.g. 5 secs, from 1.12–1.17)	Cost

Fig 4.11b   Advanced search facility of the British Pathe catalogue

WEBSITE

http://www.britishpathe.com/advanced_search.php

Although there has obviously been a strong focus in this section on what ICT can do for history, it is important to remember that the contexts which history can provide for data handling work can do much for ICT. Most of the activities in this chapter fit more than one of the requirements of the KS3 Framework for ICT.

Fig 4.12   Selected extracts from the KS3 Framework for ICT

Teaching Objectives from the KS3 Framework for ICT		
Year 7	Year 8	Year 9
Searching and selecting ● Search a variety of sources for information relevant to a task (for example, using indexes, search techniques, navigational structures and engines). ● Narrow down a search to achieve more relevant results. ● Assess the value of information from various sources to a particular task. ● Acknowledge sources of information used. **Organizing and investigating** ● In an investigation: – design and use an appropriate data handling structure to answer questions and draw conclusions; – design a questionnaire or data collection sheet to provide relevant data; – check data efficiently for errors; – investigate relationships between variables; – use software to represent data in simple graphs, charts or tables, justifying the choice of representation; – derive new information from data, for example, averages, probabilities; – check whether conclusions are plausible; – review and amend the structure and its data to answer further questions.	**Using data and information sources** ● Understand how the content and style of an information source affect its suitability for particular purposes, by considering: – its mix of fact, opinion and material designed to advertise, publicize or entertain; – the viewpoints it offers; – the clarity, accessibility and plausibility of the material. ● Devise and apply criteria to evaluate how well various information sources will support a task. ● Justify the use of particular information sources to support an investigation or presentation. **Searching and selecting** ● Extend and refine search methods to be more efficient (for example, using synonyms and AND, OR, NOT). ● Explain the advantages of the methods used by different search engines and programs to search for data in various formats.	**Using data and information sources** ● Select information sources and data systematically for an identified purpose by: – judging the reliability of the information sources; – identifying possible bias due to sampling methods; – collecting valid, accurate data efficiently; – recognizing potential misuse of collected data. **Searching and selecting** ● As part of a study, analyse high-volume quantitative and qualitative data systematically by: – exploring the data to form and test hypotheses; – identifying correlations between variables; – drawing valid conclusions and making predictions; – reviewing the process of analysis and the plausibility of the predictions or conclusions.

The example cited on pages 19–20 is reproduced again here (overleaf) as a reminder of how curriculum requirements of history and ICT can come together powerfully to help develop critical thinking. In this example, students were asked to examine sections of *The Ragged Trousered Philanthropists* by Robert Tressell. This book was published in the early 1900s as a damning indictment of the hardship of working class life in the late 1800s and early 1900s.

WEBSITE

WEBSITE

WEBSITE

The text and a facsimile of the original manuscript is available free online from the TUC's archive site, The Union Makes Us Strong (http://www.unionhistory.info/index.php). Many other relevant and fascinating documents are also available from this site. Having used the book extracts to establish one view of life at the time, students were then asked to examine the census data for various London boroughs in 1891 from the London Grid for Learning (http://www.lgfl.net/lgfl/accounts/virtualhistory/) to see if they could find evidence which supported the picture given in the book. Further useful evidence was available from the LSE Charles Booth Archive (http://booth.lse.ac.uk/). It is hard to dispute that an activity such as this constitutes rigorous history. However, the task was constructed in such a way that there were important ICT outcomes as well. Students were encouraged to summarize their findings in terms of the value of the software to the historical enquiry using the writing framework in figure 4.13.

Fig 4.13 **Framework used to help students reflect on their learning in the investigation into life in Britain c1900**

Writing frame
Living standards in London 1891

The hypothesis I was investigating was…

The 1891 census helps historians draw conclusions about the different standards of living in Greenwich and Tower Hamlets. The indicators of a poor standard of living are…

The indicators of a high standard of living are…

My research shows that in Greenwich there are…

While in Tower Hamlets the percentage of … is…

This suggests that… and …

The reason why I think this is because…

On the other hand not all the evidence was as clear-cut.

Evidence to support there being similar standards of living can be see in pie chart/bar chart…

This shows that the proportion/percentage of… whereas the proportion of… is only…

This suggests…

Overall therefore the evidence seems to show that in the areas of…

Life in… was much worse/better than life in …

Using ViewPoint software was helpful in arriving at my conclusions because…

However, I need to be cautious about my conclusions because the data set does not give complete information about standards of living. Other aspects of standards of living that I need to research further are…

The types of evidence that I need to do this are…

WEBSITE

Interpretations and the citizenship dimension

The task on Huntingdon Jail also offers the opportunity to engage with and combine issues of historical interpretations and citizenship. Tasks 2 and 3 effectively require students to hold up an apparently factual account to close scrutiny against fairly hard evidence. This skill could be very gainfully employed in the history classroom. For example, a data file relating to a particular regiment in the Great War could be used to test out some of the commonly accepted 'truths' about the Great War. Likely 'truths' to be tested would be that few officers were killed, most soldiers were volunteers and soldiers spent weeks in muddy trenches. One of the most powerful sources of data on the Great War is the Commonwealth War Graves Commission Debt of Honour Register (http://www.cwgc.org/). Similarly, Victorian prejudices about Irish immigrants (not difficult to find in contemporary newspaper reports) might be tested against actual census returns to see whether claims of a town being swamped by such immigrants were justified.

It is not difficult to see how such an approach might be employed to link history and citizenship. The same methodology might be applied to claims made in the press or other quarters about the numbers and impact of immigrants or asylum seekers in a particular area. Data files cannot assess cultural and other anxieties but they may help to address the fact that public perception of issues such as crime levels is often wildly out of step with the actual figures.

Joined up approaches using data handling – the local dimension

Finally, another history and citizenship dimension enabled by the use of ICT is the local dimension. Examining census and similar data can help students to build a personal connection between themselves and the people who lived in their locality at different times in the past. The example in figure 4.11 is focused on life in the early twentieth century. It would be quite possible to get students analysing figures on deaths from plague in 1666 and then addressing questions such as 'Was Samuel Pepys exaggerating in his diary?'

Beyond London, students could use data to examine the growth in population of cities such as Sheffield, Liverpool or Manchester in the eighteenth and nineteenth centuries. The New Opportunities Fund Digitization Programme has allowed many local archives to digitize large amounts of their collections and make them available online. Using old maps, original sources and data students could put together a picture of what their local area was like at particular times in the past.

These additional sources are now available online for students in many parts of the country. In addition, most students have access to exciting and motivating software tools which allow them to pull their findings together into impressive presentational formats. It is these dimensions that are to be explored in the next two chapters.

Chapter 5

Dare to ask 'Is the internet a valuable resource?'

In this section you will discover:

- The use of the internet must add value to the teaching and learning of history. It does not add value if it simply replicates the role of the textbook.

- The nature of the work done using the internet needs to be carefully monitored so that it complements tasks which engage a range of learning styles rather than swamping such tasks.

- Search engines can be a useful tool but they need to be used in a planned way that allows for the fact that they have weaknesses as well as uses.

- Even weak sites can be extremely useful teaching resources if used imaginatively.

- The internet can be an invaluable source of specialist knowledge unavailable anywhere else. Such material can be used as the basis for activities which allow a range of approaches and suit different learning styles.

- The internet is becoming an increasingly valuable repository of primary source material. This includes material which can be used to engage emotions – a powerful tool for making learning memorable.

- Much primary source material is unmediated and needs careful thought about how students will use it. There are some exceptions to this rule, such as the Learning Curve website.

- The internet can be an invaluable tool for local studies

- The internet can be a powerful source of historical interpretations. These include reconstructions, academic, popular and polemical interpretations. All can be used, but again they need careful consideration by the teacher as to how they will be used.

- The internet provides exciting opportunities for teachers and students to communicate their ideas about history. Email and video conferencing also provide excellent opportunities to help schools create and extend collaborative learning communities.

▌Using the internet in the history classroom

Getting value from the internet

In some respects, the question as to whether the internet is a valuable resource is answered by the thousands of students and teachers using it every day to study history and many other subjects. However, the fact that a resource is used does not necessarily mean that we are getting the maximum value from that resource. It is so easy to be seduced by the prospect of the vast amount of material 'out there'. However, if we stop and think for a moment, we might ask ourselves exactly how valuable that data resource is. Primary and secondary schools clearly taught history before the internet. By implication, they already had enough information in textbooks, library books, television programmes and so on to teach their courses. At a time when teachers (with some justification) are feeling overwhelmed by their workload, how enthusiastically should we be embracing another great pile of 'stuff'? Are we perhaps being sucked in to a rather simplistic view of the value of the internet? Terry Haydn et al (2003) note:

> *... at one level, ICT is very good at delivering things. Those who teach are, however, more aware that 'deliver' does not guarantee 'learning'. The idea that there is a necessary correlation between the volume of information available and the amount of learning that takes place can also be detected in politicians' ideas about the educational potential of the internet for pupils (see, for instance, Tony Blair in the* Guardian, *1 November 1998). In the words of John Naughton (*Observer, *22 March 1998): 'It's not every day that you encounter a member of the government who appears to understand the Net. Most politicians (Clinton, Blair, Blunkett, to name just three) see it as a kind of pipe for pumping things into schools and schoolchildren.'*

My own observations have led me to believe that when it comes to ICT in general, and the internet in particular, our expectations are simply too low. We are taken in by the simple fact that there is some material vaguely relevant to our course of study. Ofsted reports rightly upbraid us when our lessons involve students simply transferring information from one place (textbook, board, internet) to another (exercise book, printout). We need to be sure that our use of the internet helps to overcome this problem, not make it worse.

At the risk of stating the obvious, we need to treat the internet as we would treat any other resource. Primary or secondary teachers are extremely expert at quickly and astutely evaluating resources such as textbooks, library books and television programmes. The internet presents us with new opportunities and new challenges but in many ways the old challenges and issues are just as important. Thinking about the use of the internet requires some new questions and some familiar ones. For example:

➡ **Is searching for information on an historical subject a worthwhile activity?** To put this into context it is worth asking how often we send students to the library because there are a lot of history books there. And if it takes all lesson for students to make a decision about which book to use, do we regard this as a worthwhile outcome? We need to consider these points if we are planning lessons which involve students using search engines for relevant material on a particular subject.

➡️ **Why is the internet being used at all?** The internet is a repository of information, but how often do websites contribute little or nothing more than can be found in a textbook? If the website is simply replicating what can be found in a textbook, why are we using it?

➡️ **Is our goal really the accessing of information?** The fact that information exists on a website does not make it especially valid. Are we as teachers clear about what we want students to do with that information? We need to be extremely clear about why the internet is being used as the information source in a particular task. If we are not, then we run the danger of Encarta syndrome as mentioned in chapter 2. Worse still, we run the risk of frustrating and confusing our students. For example, a student looking for information on the impact of the Civil Wars of the 1640s on ordinary people will find a lot of material about the Civil Wars. Much of it, however, is likely to be about the tactics used at the Battle of Marston Moor or the efficacy of the matchlock musket rather than on the subject being investigated.

➡️ **Do we want a specific type of information?** This would seem to be a more valuable use of the web. Many websites now hold collections of original sources. Some websites might provide detailed insights into particular themes, such as military strategy or industrial technology. In this context the 'unhelpful' website on military tactics or weapons of the Civil Wars starts to become an asset rather than a problem. At the same time, in this context, the more general website becomes unhelpful as it may not hold enough detail to help students with the very specific enquiry they have been set.

➡️ **What strategies do we have to address the issue that much material on the internet is irrelevant or even unsuitable?** There is a lot of material which is highly unsuitable for students of certain ages. This might be for reasons of political bias, unsuitable content or simply the level at which the material is pitched. On the other hand, some sites which appear to be weak may actually offer us an opportunity for an interesting teaching approach. That said, a weak resource can only be a useful resource if the teacher carefully plans and prepares its use.

So the fundamental message here is that the internet should be used in the same way as other ICT resources – when it has something unique or very special to offer. Using the internet can be troublesome. For many teachers special arrangements have to be made with regard to booking rooms or exchanging rooms with colleagues. There may be a need to march a class of students some distance across the school. Then there are the technical issues, most notably very slow performance of web pages or loss of connection altogether. Then there is the vexed question of finding something on the internet suited to your particular needs. Admittedly, there are now also resources which make searching less of a lottery such as the Curriculum Online portal site

WEBSITE

(http://www.curriculumonline.gov.uk). This site contains a range of interesting features and articles but its main asset is a catalogue of resources. These can be searched by subject, Key Stage, year group, keywords and so on. The results then indicate whether the resource is free or purchasable. Most products have been reviewed by teachers. Another useful resource is the 24 Hour Museum

WEBSITE

website (http://www.24hourmuseum.org.uk). This site acts as an index or catalogue of British museums. It also has a facility to search the museums for online collections relevant to particular curriculum topics and themes. As with most resources, teachers will probably search through the wide range of available material, trial some materials, reject others, refine the most suitable and settle into a pattern of use with the materials that suit them best. This is good, sensible practice. However, one word of caution – it's worth searching for materials from time to time as new material is emerging all the time, and is often carefully chosen for its ability to inform, entertain and surprise.

All of the above are serious concerns. They should not preclude using the internet, but should ensure that when we do, we are getting maximum return from this investment. The rest of this section is devoted to looking at examples of how the internet has been or could be used to maximize this return.

Searching for information

I have already raised some of the concerns about lessons in which students use search engines to locate material for an historical enquiry. Many teachers will know from bitter experience that the searching process can be considerably more difficult and time consuming than the actual historical enquiry itself. A good example of this was a recent search by some primary school students working on life in Victorian times. After keying in this search title – 'life in Victorian times' – some promising looking results appeared. The Victorian Web (http://www.victorianweb.org) appeared to fit the bill exactly, especially from its attractively visual front page. However, a few forays into the content of the site will reveal that it is aimed at the undergraduate student and is pitched way too high for the average primary school student. Another website which appeared was, not surprisingly, Victorian Times (http://www.victoriantimes.org). This site is far more suitable at first sight, particularly since it has a clever filtering device which allows the user to indicate their age and educational level and tailors the results of searches accordingly. That said, even this site caused some scratching of heads because it is a collection of primary source material. In this particular instance the students were after more authored information to give them a general picture of living conditions.

Clarity of purpose

Eventually, many of them found the Victorian Britain link on the Spartacus website (http://www.spartacus.schoolnet.co.uk/). This site is perhaps the most comprehensive source of encyclopedia style authored material for history on the internet. The teacher had this site in mind when setting the task to the students, so it does raise the question of why students were not simply directed to this site, and maybe even directed to particular pages on the site using instructions or pre-prepared bookmarks. The teacher in this instance was caught in a classic halfway house. Students were asked to use search engines in the hope that they might find some new and interesting sites. There was also an aim that students would develop searching and decision-making skills, as well as developing their historical knowledge and understanding once the relevant information had been located from the internet. This turned out to be a pretty tall order, mainly because of the time needed to search, locate and evaluate sites *and then* use them in the historical enquiry.

The electronic worksheet

So in this type of use of the internet, the key is to define clearly what the core purpose of the activity is. In the instance described above the core purpose was actually to use rather than locate information about living conditions in

WEBSITE

WEBSITE

WEBSITE

Victorian times. Thus, the most effective approach would probably have been to provide students with a few pre-selected websites and some guidance on what information they were looking for. One of the most effective ways of doing this is to create an electronic worksheet in which the link to the relevant site is clickable. This avoids the potential hazard of incorrect typing of addresses. The electronic worksheet is simply a word processor file which is saved as read-only or as a web page. Figure 5.1 below is an example of such a resource for a study on Victorian times. The Bourne Middle School in Bourne, Massachusetts, USA has created a similar electronic worksheet on Ancient Greece (http://www.bourne.k12.ma.us/BMS/lweeks/Ancient%20Greek%20WebQuest/ancient_greece_webquest.htm). It is worth noting that the more commonly used term in the USA for an electronic worksheet is a web quest. It is well worth using a search engine for web quests on a range of topics that have been created by other schools, as it may well save you the time and effort of creating one yourself.

WEBSITE

Fig 5.1   **Part of an electronic worksheet on Victorian times. The word processor file can be saved as a web page and then the web addresses will automatically open the web page when clicked. If you want students to work on particular websites this is a very effective tool**

CD–ROM Ch 5/Life in Victorian Times
Word doc

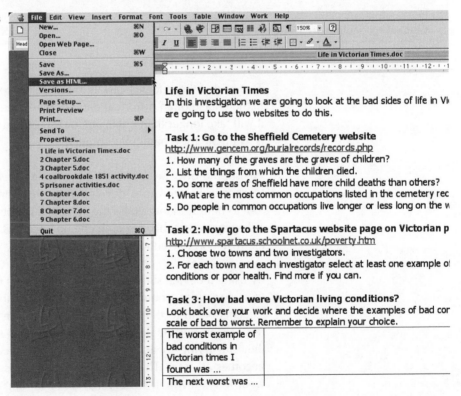

Using search engines

Of course, all of this does not mean that search engines should never be used, simply that they should be harnessed and their uses and vagaries planned for. This means planning in terms of history and ICT. Searching a range of websites is an activity that fits well with many aspects of the national curriculum for ICT in KS2 and KS3, as well as familiarizing students with the process of assessing potential sources of information in history.

> **Nat. Curr.** Ofsted
>
> **Finding things out**
> 1. Pupils should be taught:
>   a) to talk about what information they need and how they can find and use it
>   b) how to prepare information for development using ICT, including selecting suitable sources, finding information, classifying it and checking it for accuracy
>   c) to interpret information, to check it is relevant and reasonable and to think about what might happen if there were any errors or omissions.
>
> **National curriculum orders for ICT KS2**

> **Nat. Curr.** Ofsted
>
> **Finding things out**
> 1. Pupils should be taught:
>   a) to be systematic in considering the information they need and to discuss how it will be used
>   b) how to obtain information well matched to purpose by selecting appropriate sources, using and refining search methods and questioning the plausibility and value of the information found
>   c) how to collect, enter, analyse and evaluate quantitative and qualitative information, checking its accuracy.
>
> **National curriculum orders for ICT KS3**

That said, if the students' task is to search for, locate, evaluate and use websites in the course of an historical enquiry then time allowances should be made as it will take longer than if they are only required to report back on what material is available for a particular enquiry.

We should also be aware that evaluating websites is not always easy. One teacher in Bradford has developed an extremely useful pro forma evaluation tool to help students assess the value of websites on a number of levels. Using a device such as this, a search engine becomes a more focused tool rather than an invitation for random surfing.

By using a device such as figure 5.2, websites that are not actually well suited to a particular enquiry then become valuable resources. This is because students begin to think about what the nature of their enquiry is, so in some respects an unsuitable website actually helps students to clarify exactly what they are trying to achieve. Therefore the weakness of the website actually becomes an asset. This is all part of the process of helping students to become what Terry Haydn in *History, ICT and Learning in the Secondary School* (2003) calls mature users of the internet:

Recent inspection evidence shows that school history has enabled some younger pupils to develop into mature users of the internet, but there is also evidence that many older pupils have a poor understanding of the value and status of information on the internet. Given its significance, it would be a dereliction of responsibility not to consider how school history might contribute to the nurturing of school leavers who can use the internet intelligently.

> *… Mature use of the internet is not just a question of being able to search efficiently to locate information, helpful though this skill is. It is also about helping pupils to develop the 'media literacy' which is an important facet of education for citizenship. The vast, confusing and contradictory range of sources of information on the internet can be an invaluable asset in developing in pupils … a historical cast of mind … by requiring pupils to think about which procedures a historian would use to try and 'get at the truth' in the face of such difficulties. In the era of spin doctors, media manipulation, sound bite politics and information overload … one of the questions which history departments might ask is to what extent, after 9, 11, or 13 years of school history, their pupils are mature users of the internet.*

Fig 5.2   **A website evaluation sheet produced by Dan Moorhouse, head of history at Laisterdyke High School, Bradford. The sheet was for an exercise in which students had to assess the value of websites they found in terms of their usefulness for an enquiry on the causes of the Civil Wars in the 1630s–40s**

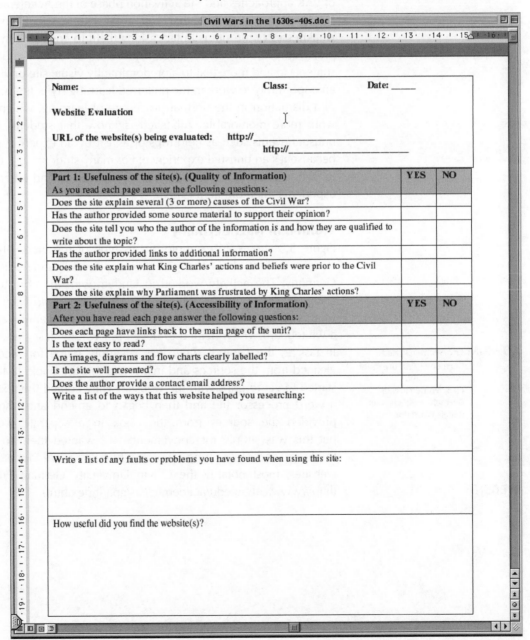

▌Making a website into a task

In the previous chapter a reference was made to the value of the weak site. Although this may seem contradictory, in fact it is not. Students are always interested in an activity which may appear to be slightly subversive or which challenges the natural order of things. The internet provides many opportunities for such activities, most often by its very weaknesses. There are so many websites on the internet that cover aspects of history in the most general of terms, and are all too often much weaker than the average textbook or library book. Equally, there are many websites that are potentially useful but terribly daunting to their potential audience because they are too dense in content and visually unappealing. The value of the internet in this particular context is that it provides a ready to criticize resource. The poor quality of many websites means that they would only be found published on the free medium of the internet as they would not make it past the quality control mechanisms of publishers. Another asset is that these resources are, of course, electronic. This makes them ideally suited to an activity in which students put right the flaws in them. In one sense this is of course the complete reversal of the main precepts of VAK approaches and the activation phase of the Accelerated Learning Cycle. However, the very fact that you are asking students to acknowledge the weaknesses of the site is in fact asking them to engage with a resource in their preferred learning style, albeit by a somewhat unorthodox route. Asking students to add more text to a predominantly visual site or vice versa is in effect an opportunity to work in the preferred learning style. It is also a good example of a disruption in the normal procedure of learning, which in fact makes the work more memorable. All teachers know that students tend to remember unusual events such as field trips or a visit by an expert. A great part of this is because it's an unusual experience. For many students, use of the internet is no longer an unusual experience and so we need to find other ways to make the experience memorable for them.

Women in Nazi Germany

Figure 5.3 shows an example of this type of resource. I have used it to get students to think about changing views on the role and status of women in Nazi Germany. The activity worked in tandem with the core textbook they were using on Nazi Germany (Hite & Hinton, *Weimar and Nazi Germany*, Hodder Murray). The two images from the textbook were scanned and projected on to a whiteboard which helped to develop a whole-class discussion on task 1(a). In task 2, the capture sheet was a simple frame for recording information gleaned from the sources and information in the book. In task 3, the students started to get to grips with the website. They copied the text from the site into a word processor file and then began to amend and improve it. I actually provided the sources from the book in a separate word processor file but this was simply for convenience – I wanted them to spend more time thinking and less time typing. Images were located from various websites, most notably the Calvin University German Propaganda Archive (http://www.calvin.edu/academic/cas/gpa/index.htm).

CD–ROM Ch 5/Women in Nazi Germany – Capture sheet Word doc and Ch 5/Women in Nazi Germany – Policies and Beliefs Word doc

WEBSITE

Fig 5.3   Task sheet on women in Nazi Germany

CD-ROM Ch 5/Women in Nazi Germany
–Task sheet Word doc

An important point to mention here is that this was not the end of the task. I also got students to establish the downsides of life in Nazi Germany for women, via a series of further tasks. In the process, they created their own improved web page on this subject. The majority simply revised the original web page in a word processor file and then saved it as a web page. Some took the time and trouble to load their work into desktop publishing or web authoring software. All were able to use their work as evidence of key skills communication and ICT, as well as history. Crucially, however, there was one final element in the history process – after this task, I introduced students to a further range of printed material from history journals and textbooks which suggested that the story of women in Nazi Germany was not only one of victim hood. The up-to-date research suggests a more complex picture in which some women gained real opportunities and many women supported many aspects of the regime's policies. Having studied this new knowledge, students were then sent back to update their revised web pages further.

Complete history of the Great War?
Clearly this example involved a lot of work and is relatively complex, as it should be for a task carried out by students at AS level. The basic principle, however, is entirely applicable to many other circumstances. Another profitable site of material which is ripe for revision by students is the one-sided view of history which can often be found on websites. I have used a site that advertises a particular CD-ROM as an example of this, A2ZCDS. The relevant page of the site (http://www.a2zcds.com/DetailInfo.asp?pid=63&qid=2) was advertising a CD-ROM on the Great War. It claims to provide comprehensive coverage of the Great War and yet the selection of thumbnail images suggests that there is a heavily American centric focus in this particular history. The task in this instance, which Year 9 students had to perform, was to redesign the selection of thumbnail images. Their brief was to select images which reflected the entirety

WEBSITE

WEBSITE
WEBSITE

of the war in their opinion. There are many excellent sources of Great War images. The two used in this activity were the World War I Document Archive (http://www.blakearchive.org.uk/mirrors/www.lib.byu.edu:80/~rdh/wwi/) and Photos of the Great War (http://www.gwpda.org/photos/greatwar.htm).

Rewriting the Vikings and Tudors

WEBSITE

Reworking websites is an activity that need not be confined to sites with flaws. For example, the BBC's Schools material on the Vikings (http://www.bbc.co.uk/schools/vikings/) is sensibly designed to appeal to the relatively young student. In some cases even these pages might be seen as too heavy for a young reader. Thus, an ideal task might be to divide the various sections of the site between groups of students and ask them to come up with shorter versions of the material in each section to make it easier for their classmates. They could simply re-present their work or, as with the AS students,

WEBSITE

create new word processor documents or web pages. The 'adult' BBC site on the Vikings (http://www.bbc.co.uk/history/ancient/vikings/) offers many opportunities to take the task in the opposite direction, with students adding photographs, maps, plans and even archaeological findings to enhance the materials.

Fig 5.4   **Menu page of the BBC's KS2 resources on the Vikings showing the topic areas covered**

This principle could be applied particularly effectively with a topic such as the Tudors, taking advantage of the fact that the Tudors are studied at KS2 and KS3. Students at KS3 might be encouraged to revise a KS2 site 'upwards' to meet their requirements, or 'downwards' to be suitable for a KS2 audience. KS2 students could be set the same challenge. A web page such as the links page of Stretton Handley primary school in Derbyshire

WEBSITE

(http://www.strettonhandley.derbyshire.sch.uk/) provides an excellent selection of sites which teachers could use to allocate different sites to different students according to their aptitudes and abilities.

WEBSITE

One of the great hazards with using sites this way is that many of the most useful sites (that is ones which have serious weaknesses) are prone to disappear from one year to the next. This can be deeply frustrating if you have not saved the relevant pages to your own computer using the 'File – Save As' function of your browser. One possible source of help is the Internet Archive (http://www.archive.org/). This American project attempts to archive websites in the same way that other archives collect and preserve documents. There is no guarantee that your lost site will be preserved here but it's worth a try.

Picking the brains of the experts: Access to material not available otherwise

It would be a great waste of what the internet has to offer to concentrate only on its weaknesses! One of its greatest assets is the facility it provides to give students and teachers access to expert knowledge on a range of topics taught in primary and secondary history. It would be tempting to see the value of the internet in the next few examples as providing access to source material. Of course, each example does show this; however, in these examples there is a slightly more subtle point. Accessing the source material in these instances is helpful and motivating, but the source material itself is rather challenging. Without some expert mediation it is unlikely that students or even teachers will be able to extract the full meaning from it. Short of inviting an expert round to interpret each source, the internet seems the only realistic option for introducing students to the process of decoding source material that needs expert knowledge. It is in this area that ICT provides another opportunity for connecting learning. In this instance the tasks are connecting between the content of the resources and the analytical processes being used to interpret those sources.

An Ancient Egyptian party

Using the internet, a student in KS2 studying ancient civilizations such as Egypt or Greece, or Roman Britain, can look at all sorts of everyday objects which these people used. The British Museum has a main website and also a collection of photographs of objects which can be searched through a website called Compass. There is a more accessible version of the Compass site called Children's Compass. Using Children's Compass, for example, you can see Ancient Egyptians having a party (see figure 5.5). This is a classic example in which the expert knowledge of the curators at the British Museum has been made available to teachers and students who would not be able to visit the museum or talk to the relevant curator. Resources like this open up exciting opportunities for a range of enquiries such as:

➡ How did the Ancient Egyptians enjoy themselves?

➡ How hard was life in Ancient Egypt?

➡ How do we know about the ordinary lives of Ancient Egyptians?

This last question is clearly on a different level of challenge from the other two, as it is getting young students to think not so much about what we know but how we know it. This means looking at the source but also the techniques used to draw inferences from the sources and how historians turn these into evidence to support an historical interpretation. Students could copy images from the website into their own reports or presentations and then explain to the class how and why a particular artefact they have chosen is useful to the historian in explaining how the Ancient Egyptians lived. Clearly this is very challenging, but the resource makes it possible to access the source material in a range of different learning styles and also to present understanding in a variety of ways. The visual elements of this source are self-evident, but the auditory learner will gain much from the accompanying text. If the teacher is feeling very brave, perhaps the kinesthetic learners might be allowed to explain the party scene by acting it out and bringing it to life (up to a point!). Without resources such as Children's Compass, it is hard to see how such an approach would be possible at all.

Fig 5.5   **Screen shot from the British Museum's Children's Compass online resource**

WEBSITE   http://www.thebritishmuseum.ac.uk/childrenscompass/index.html

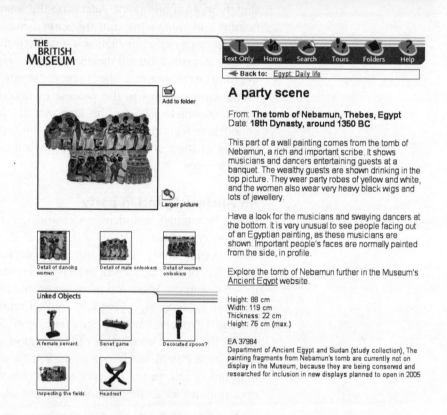

How did the Great War affect the soldiers?

In figure 5.6 the activity is different from the task on the Egyptians set out above but the core principle is the same. The collection of paintings on the Art of the First World War website is extremely powerful, but many of the paintings need expert commentary in order to appreciate their full meaning and power. This allows students to connect with the source material and indeed the history of the war itself through emotional intelligence. This can be one of the most powerful forms of intelligence, and learning experiences that tap into emotions are generally ones which stay in the minds of students.

Fig 5.6   An activity using the internet to explore original source material and expert commentary

CD–ROM Ch 4/Great War art poem activity Word doc

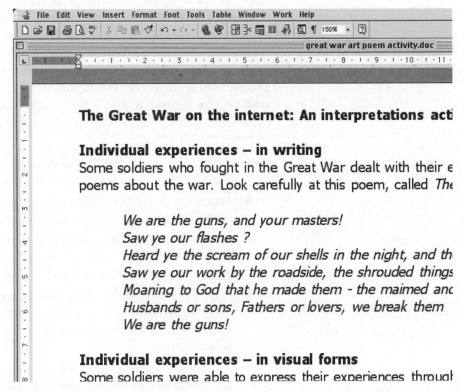

The Great War on the internet: An interpretations acti

Individual experiences – in writing
Some soldiers who fought in the Great War dealt with their e
poems about the war. Look carefully at this poem, called *The*

> *We are the guns, and your masters!*
> *Saw ye our flashes ?*
> *Heard ye the scream of our shells in the night, and th*
> *Saw ye our work by the roadside, the shrouded things*
> *Moaning to God that he made them - the maimed anc*
> *Husbands or sons, Fathers or lovers, we break them*
> *We are the guns!*

Individual experiences – in visual forms
Some soldiers were able to express their experiences throug

The task offers opportunities to study a range of sources and to use the expert commentaries that accompany each painting to gain a deep and meaningful understanding of the individual painters' experiences. The task also offers the opportunity to use a range of ICT tools. The most exciting is for students to create the actual double page spread using desktop publishing software. They can copy their chosen painting for the website to their publication, perhaps adding a caption to their painting which explains how it complements the poem.

The extension task is just as important in terms of historical balance – seeing that there is another side to the war to which poetry and paintings alone do not do justice. It also raises an important point about the value of Amazon and other sites which sell books. Few students in Years 9–11 have the time, enthusiasm or intellectual stamina required to read books such as the one referred to in the task. However, the reviews and synopses in these sites give students a sense of the core arguments being set out in the book. This is another good example of using the internet as a shortcut to the ideas of the experts!

Obviously, the approach in figure 5.6 is in no way confined to the topic area of the Great War. It could just as easily be applied to the diary of a child evacuated in the Second World War. It could be used in the context of the experiences of an African enslaved and transported across the Atlantic in the eighteenth century. It could also apply to the equally sensitive subject of the Holocaust. There are many poor sites on the Holocaust but also some good ones. A good starting point is the Cybrary of the Holocaust (http://www.remember.org/).

WEBSITE

WEBSITE

One final resource worth mentioning under this heading is the BBC Radio 4 history website (http://www.bbc.co.uk/radio4/history/). Radio 4 produces a large amount of very high quality programming on historical subjects. For most students, a highbrow Radio 4 programme might not be the most exciting experience they will ever have. This is where the Radio 4 website becomes invaluable. The site summarizes most programmes and usually includes a range of visual materials. The most interesting point is that Radio 4 history programmes tend to concentrate on slightly unusual themes and issues. In addition, the website not only allows users to listen to programmes at their convenience, but also to browse within the programme. Thus, within this resource it is possible to:

➡ Listen to a section of the series *Making history*, which addresses the question 'Are television costume dramas accurate?'

➡ Access the series *The People's D-Day* to study the contribution of civilians to D-Day 1944 and its impact on them.

➡ Use the series *Why did we do that?* to examine the roots of everyday activities and actions such as why we consider something good to be 'the best thing since sliced bread'.

➡ Study extracts from the series *The Roman Way* and *The Norman Way* which focus strongly on the lives of ordinary people and the ways in which historians and archaeologists have been able to reconstruct their lives.

➡ Use the series *Heroes and Villains* to examine how historical figures are seen very differently in different countries. As former Monty Python member memorably asks:

> *As for Attila the Hun, OK, so he murdered his brothers, slaughtered thousands of Christians and nearly extinguished Western civilization, but that doesn't make him a bad person, does it? Well, if you come from Hungary it makes him quite a good person – the meanest fighting machine to ever break out of the Hungarian Steppes – and they're rather proud of him, even to the point of reconstructing his palace.*

➡ Gain an overview of relatively poorly resourced areas such as medieval Africa from the summaries and web links in the material that supports the series *The Story of Africa* (this is actually a BBC World Service site –

WEBSITE

http://www.bbc.co.uk/worldservice/africa/features/storyofafrica/).

▌ Accessing primary source material and archives

Another way in which the internet can make itself valuable is in helping teachers and students to access original sources from a period or geographical area. The use of historical sources has been a common feature of history teaching in primary and secondary schools for over 20 years. However, the sources we have used have tended to be the short extracts which appear in a textbook. These have generally been accompanied by sequences of questions asking students about them. All of this is worthy stuff but a textbook rarely has the time or space to investigate a collection of source material and use sources the way a true historian uses them – to build a story.

The internet now provides us with such opportunities. There are two broad categories of websites that specialize in original sources. Some sites are primarily conveyors of source material and leave it to the user to determine their use. Others are much more mediated and have already developed an architecture of activities or resources. I have sometimes categorized these two types in the past as 'Stuff sites' and 'What to do with stuff' sites. It's a somewhat crude categorization but it does help to sort out priorities and decide which of the many archive sites on the internet are suitable for your students and your purposes. Let's look at some examples of each type of resource.

Archive sites without mediation

These are sites which concentrate on collecting and helping users to access primary source material. These collections usually have a number of valuable features which allow teachers and students to make use of these sources for a variety of purposes.

- ➡ A collection of source material not easily available via any other medium.
- ➡ Organization of sources under topic headings.
- ➡ A search feature that makes the location of suitable material relatively easy.
- ➡ The ability to copy sections of text or images to allow teachers or students to use them for their own purposes.
- ➡ Expert commentary from archivists or curators which help us to get the most from the source (an issue explored above in the section 'Picking the brains of the experts').

Archives of visual sources

One powerful use of archives is to locate a single iconic image or a collection of images which simply give students a sense of what the people, buildings and everyday paraphernalia of Roman Colchester, Tudor Oxford, Civil War Chester, Victorian Leeds or 1930s Berlin looked like. Such images or collections of images make excellent resources for starter sessions in which teachers can pose questions, ask students to speculate intelligently and ask questions which they themselves can then investigate. They can also be powerful ways to help students develop and improve memory. We know that for most students (indeed non-students as well) visual images are generally more memorable than words. Trying to link key points to visual images can be a highly effective way to drive learning. The internet provides extensive sources of powerful visual material to make such activities possible.

The British Museum Children's Compass site has already been referred to as a possible site for such visual materials. Another source of historical visual material is the commercial picture libraries. These are online catalogues of visual images designed to help picture researchers in publishing and other media sectors to quickly and easily locate images. A search on a topic will usually turn up a wide range of images (depending on the parameters of the search, of course). It also turns up a range of images from unexpected sources such as stills from movies or news documentaries, or newspaper reports of local re-enactment groups. The Hulton Archive (http://www.hultonarchive.com, now hosted on the archival section of http://editorial.gettyimages.com) is particularly strong on American material and also this type of media based image. Other archives which have strong collections of images are the Mary

WEBSITE

WEBSITE

WEBSITE

WEBSITE

Evans Picture Library (http://www.maryevans.com/). The Mary Evans archive contains a lot of reconstruction drawings of past periods. Many of these are anachronistic but even these can be useful in helping students to see how different periods were interpreted differently at different times. A number of different partners all contribute to the Heritage Image Partnership website (http://www.heritage-images.com/). The collections on this site range very widely, but tend to be more academic than the previous two collections because the majority of images come from some of the major British cultural institutions, including the British Library, the National Archives and the Science Museum. A final resource which must be mentioned is the National Portrait Gallery (http://www.npg.org.uk/). By its very nature, this collection is invaluable as it provides us with the closest we have to a likeness of many historic figures that lived before the age of photography. In each case with these sites, the images are on sale and publishers must pay copyright fees to use them. However, for most teachers the free downloadable preview quality images are of sufficient quality for use as starters, perhaps projected on to a whiteboard from the website.

Text and visual sources

Another good reason for using collections of original sources is to help students gain an insight into the views, feelings, cultural values and prejudices of a particular period. For fairly obvious reasons, the majority of collections of text sources suitable for use in schools tend to be from the nineteenth and twentieth centuries and found on British sites.

Women in the Second World War

For example, the Sainsbury Virtual Museum website (http://www.j-sainsbury.co.uk/museum/museum.htm) has an interesting collection of notes sent out from Sainsbury's head office to branch managers during the course of the Second World War. Of course head office sent out thousands of messages and instructions, but Sainsbury has collected a select few which concern the employment and treatment of women in the store during the war years. Figure 5.7 below is an extract from this resource. What is fascinating in the case of this source is the way in which a note about the staffing of a grocery store can inadvertently reveal so much about contemporary attitudes towards women.

Fig 5.7   **One of the letters written to Sainsbury branch managers during the Second World War**

WEBSITE

http://www.j-sainsbury.co.uk/museum/1939.htm

Click on the document 'Engagement of Females, 7 September 1939, typed copy' to locate the letter.

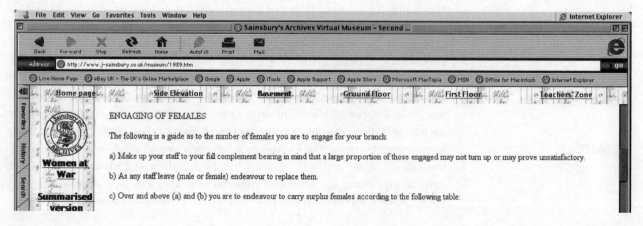

The low expectations of women and the unsympathetic attitude towards them can be seen in figure 5.7, written in the very earliest stages of the war. The extract shown here is one of a series of messages which end in 1944. The later messages reveal a distinctly different tone towards women workers in many respects, including such relatively modern innovations as child care and the extension of pension rights to women. That said, there are still many references within the messages of deeply entrenched attitudes towards women. This collection of sources provides teachers at KS2 or KS3 with plenty of opportunities for teaching about the home front in the Second World War. The first source could simply be used as an example of attitudes to women as a starter. A range of other sources could also be used to study the experience of women allowing students to then assess the extent of change in attitudes. An ideal source for such an investigation would be the Imperial War Museum's online multimedia collections (http://www.iwmcollections.org.uk/civilians/). Even more tightly focused on the school student audience is HOLNET (http://www.holnet.org.uk) which is short for history of London on the internet. This site contains a wide range of documents, letters, photographs and diaries on London during the war. HOLNET also has excellent resources on the Victorian period in London, with materials based on the work of Charles Booth and other Victorian social investigators of the later 1800s. At the other end of the country the Gateshead Archives have produced a resource with a similar philosophy called Westall's War (http://www.westallswar.org.uk/).

WEBSITE

WEBSITE

WEBSITE

The Irish famine

There are, however, some notable exceptions. One topic that has not always been easy to fit into the national curriculum history programmes of study is the Irish famine. Despite this, many teachers understandably feel that this catastrophic event is one which should be tackled in history courses. There are many excellent websites on the famine. One in particular that gets across a sense of how the press covered the famine is Views of the Famine (http://vassun.vassar.edu/~sttaylor/FAMINE/). This is an excellent example of a collection of original sources – text and image – which saves the teacher the job of researching and categorizing relevant material. This site contains far more than newspaper articles. It contains letters written to the various newspapers featured and also features advertisements from the time. Many of these advertisements are for ships to emigrate to North America. Another site that looks at the famine in a similar way is Interpreting the Irish Famine (http://www.people.virginia.edu/~eas5e/Irish/Famine.html). This covers much of the same ground as the previous site but adds a number of interesting alternative perspectives, particularly the Irish American perspective. The sources in these sites are heartrendingly poignant and are also vibrant with historical meaning – they allow students to get an insight into what people wrote, but more importantly into how people felt.

WEBSITE

WEBSITE

American history

In the same way that British history has embraced the technology of the internet, so has American history and American cultural institutions. At Calvin University, students can find one of the most comprehensive and useful sites on the propaganda of the Nazi period at the German Propaganda Archive (http://www.calvin.edu/academic/cas/gpa/index.htm). This site contains a huge range of text and visual propaganda material. It really does give an insight into the saturation propaganda of the Nazi regime and of the ideologies that

WEBSITE

WEBSITE

WEBSITE

propaganda was trying to spread. No less impressive is the collection of online resources at the US National Archives & Records Administration (http://www.archives.gov/index.html). The catalogues of NARA can be searched from this site, and many thousands of its records have been digitized for viewing. Most usefully, however, the archivists at NARA have collected selected documents to mark key events in US history and/or to support topics widely taught in US history classes. With the rising popularity of US history at GCSE and AS/A2 level, these resources can be extremely valuable. Currently NARA has a dramatic collection of material on the Brown verses Topeka Board of Education court case, which proved to be a landmark in the black American civil rights campaign. The Library of Congress (http://www.loc.gov/) is also a massive and impressive resource for studying US history. Its American Memory database allows users to search a vast collection of text, audio and visual material on key themes in US history.

▌ Archive sites with an educational dimension

All of the sites listed above offer tremendous opportunities to teachers. On the other hand, they all require some degree of input from the teacher. This is why a number of archives, museums and galleries have worked hard to put together 'ready to use' resources designed to help teachers use sources with relatively little preparation.

These usually come in two broad types: HOLNET, previously mentioned, is a good example of one type. Here the resource material stands alone and can be used in whatever way the teacher wishes. However, there is a supporting teachers' zone that contains important briefing notes for teachers along with suggestions and downloadable resources that teachers can use with students to get the most from the HOLNET site. Most of the major museums and galleries have teacher materials to support their online collections.

WEBSITE

WEBSITE

The other type of site is one in which the sources and activities are integrated into a ready to use resource. There are relatively few examples of these sites. One example is the British Library's Teacher's Area (http://www.bl.uk/services/learning/teachers.html). However, the most high profile example of such a site is probably The National Archives Learning Curve site (http://learningcurve.gov.uk/). This is a huge sprawling site which offers a range of different types of resources. The most widely used are the snapshots. These are small-scale activities focused on a small number of sources which guide students towards an understanding of the sources, how they are used and an insight into the wider issue which is being covered in the snapshot task.

Fig 5.8a   Part of the Learning Curve Snapshot entitled 'How did Henry VIII get up in the morning?' By using key sources and carefully constructed tasks the snapshot explores how Henry VIII used rituals and his own personality to stamp his authority on his people

WEBSITE   http://learningcurve.gov.uk/snapshots/snapshot23/snapshot23.htm

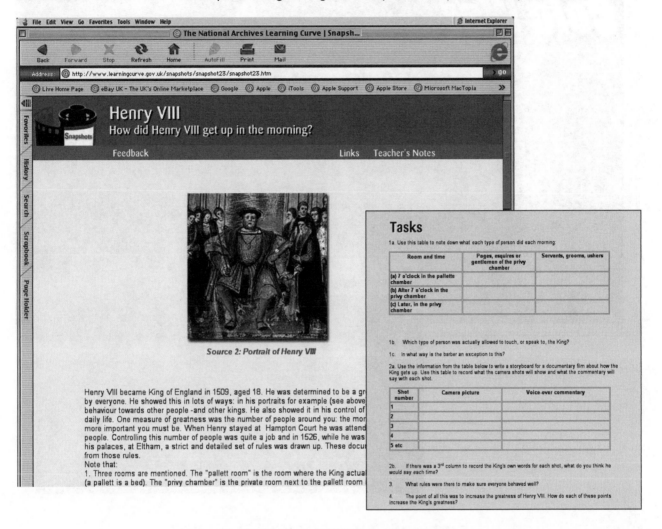

Other sections of the Learning Curve site include the 'Focus On ...' sections and the exhibitions. 'The Focus On ...' sections are designed to help students and teachers explore key sources, such as Domesday Book or key types of sources such as cartoons, letters or censuses. The exhibitions are large-scale resources that cover large topics in some detail. Although very large, they are broken up into smaller component parts and so are designed to be used very flexibly. In many respects the Learning Curve pulls together many of the key elements of web based resources for history. It provides focused material on topics generally taught in primary and secondary schools. It provides access to a range of sources difficult to access anywhere else. It provides expert guidance and commentary on the original sources to help students and teachers get the most from them. It contains a teaching structure which is very focused on enhancing students' understanding of key issues. Finally, it uses technology to interest and engage students wherever possible. In some cases, the use of technology may simply be a word processed worksheet. At the other end of the scale students can, in several exhibitions, create their own online exhibition using the material on the site.

Fig 5.8b Extracts from the Learning Curve Exhibition on the Cold War. The front page shows the structure of the exhibition. It is based around key questions and each of these key questions is further divided into case studies

WEBSITE   http://www.learningcurve.gov.uk/coldwar/default.htm

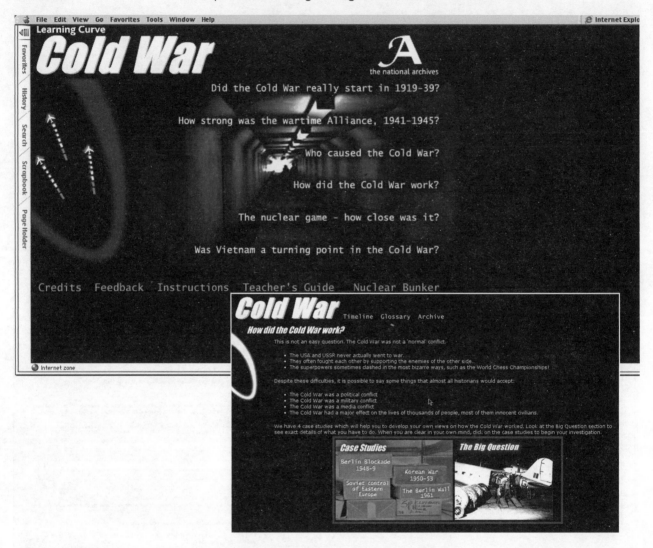

Using the internet for local studies

Another way in which the internet can provide real value is in local studies. Students at KS2 or KS3 who want to study their local environment and how it has changed over time now have easy access to some powerful source material. Students in Liverpool, for example, could study their local area or a well-known part of the city, such as the Albert Dock. The Ordnance Survey

WEBSITE

website (http://www.ordnancesurvey.co.uk/) can give them a view of the area as it is today, and the linked historic maps resource can take them to the same area in the nineteenth century – the heyday of the Albert Dock. Having gained this bigger picture, students can use the Mersey Gateway website

WEBSITE

(http://www.mersey-gateway.org.uk) to look for stories and original sources about the Albert Dock. From this point the wonderful potential of electronic resources can be exploited. Students could copy the various maps into presentations of their own and then label them, annotate them or even add audio-visual commentaries to explain how the Albert Dock, or indeed any other area, has changed over a given period of time. For different eras it might be possible to locate recorded oral histories, or have students reading out written testimonies. It is quite possible to link this type of work with some of the type of activities set out in the previous section on data handling, particularly activities involving local census data. These possibilities are explored further in the next chapter of the book.

Merseyside is far from unique in terms of having this kind of support. The neighbouring industrial North West is well served by the Manchester Archives site, Spinning the Web (http://www.spinningtheweb.org.uk/). The Port Cities resources (http://www.portcities.org.uk/) include the Mersey Gateway site but

WEBSITE
WEBSITE

Fig 5.9a **Present day OS map of the Albert Dock in Liverpool. Once located (usually**
(left) **via a postcode) you can then click on 'Historic maps' and see the same area in earlier OS maps**

WEBSITE   http://www.ordnancesurvey.co.uk/oswebsite/getamap

Fig 5.9b **Extract from the Mersey Gateway resource on the Albert Dock**
(right)

WEBSITE   http://www.mersey-gateway.org.uk/server.php?show=ConNarrative.131
&chapterId=892

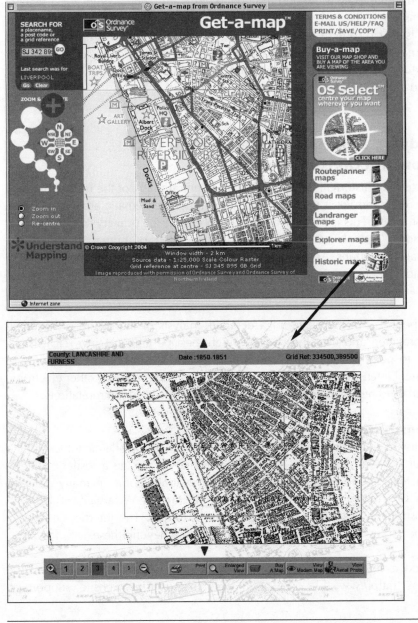

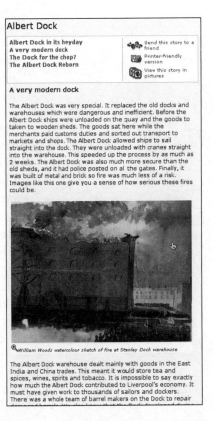

WEBSITE

WEBSITE

WEBSITE

WEBSITE

WEBSITE

also cover Bristol, London, Southampton and Hartlepool. The University of Aston's site on Central Birmingham (http://web.archive.org/web/20040211101813/http://www.cs.aston.ac.uk/oldbrum/) is a good starting point for this city. The North East of England gets good coverage from the Tomorrow's History site (http://www.tomorrows-history.com/). Rural areas might well find suitable material and local web links from the University of Reading's Museum of English Rural Life website (http://www.ruralhistory.org/index.html).

Another dimension that the internet can help with is the impact of immigration on particular areas and communities. The Moving Here website (http://www.movinghere.org.uk/) contains a vast wealth of resources which allow users to explore the experiences of migrants from different communities to different parts of Britain. This can be a particularly valuable resource for students whose roots lie in communities that are sometimes marginalized by resources which focus on the grand sweep of history.

These are just a couple of examples which illustrate the vast wealth of material being made available by the UK's holders of archives and artefacts. The National Lottery and other sources of funding have made it possible for many museums and archives to develop their online collections. The 24 Hour Museum (http://www.24hourmuseum.co.uk) is the central point for a teacher looking for collections on a particular theme. The critical point for teachers here is that resources such as these are much more than simply sources of information. The web based resources of museums and archives offer a number of extra dimensions which allow the ICT to provide the much sought after added value.

▌Studying academic interpretations and reconstructions of the past

The study of historical interpretations is a central plank of the history national curriculum and yet it is also arguably the most problematic area for teachers and students. This is perhaps a greater problem in the primary school than the secondary school, because a smaller proportion of primary teachers are specialist historians. As a result, the study of historical interpretation can seem intimidating and arcane. It must be said that it is just as intimidating and arcane for many secondary history specialists.

This book is not the place for a detailed analysis of the nature of historical interpretation and how the concept might best be taught. However, it is the place to point out the ways in which the internet can be a useful source of historical interpretations to study and how it can be used with other electronic resources to help students access and evaluate historical interpretations.

Reconstructions

It is easy to associate historical interpretations with dry, academic tomes written by out of touch scholars who have never had to engage a restless student. However, we should remember that interpretations come in many different forms. One of the most accessible is the reconstruction. We are all familiar with reconstruction drawings which appear in textbooks. The internet contains a number of resources that allow us to go one step beyond these.

WEBSITE

A good example is the American Public Broadcasting Service series on the Vikings (http://www.pbs.org/wgbh/nova/vikings/). The website supports a television series on the Vikings with a wide range of links, commentaries and other helpful resources. However, the jewel in the crown is the facility to explore a Viking village. The village is an accurate scale model built using archaeological data and then brought to life using the latest television camerawork. You can 'travel' around different parts of the village. What is also incredibly useful is the commentary which informs the user about how the scenes were shot.

WEBSITE

It's also easy to get a good feel for life in Ancient Egypt by looking at the Manchester Museum's site on the city of Kahun (http://kahun.man.ac.uk/). This takes the original findings of the archaeologist Flinders Petrie, updates them and makes them accessible to a modern audience with articles, diagrams and virtual reality reconstructions. A similar approach is taken by the website

WEBSITE

Eternal Egypt (http://www.eternalegypt.org/). Both employ text, visuals and reconstructions but which are solidly based on original academic work.

If you are interested in the Romans then there is a wealth of material on the web, seemingly because American scholars are so interested in them. The ArtsEdNet site on the forum of Trajan in Rome

WEBSITE

(http://www.getty.edu/artsednet/Exhibitions/Trajan/index.html) contains a similar combination of resources to the Viking site previously mentioned. It has information and galleries of photographs of Trajan's forum in Rome as it appears now. It also has virtual reality reconstructions of the forum at its peak and, crucially, it also has descriptions of how artists, technologists and archaeologists came together to create the virtual reality reconstructions.

Students looking at the Tudor period in Britain are also able to access some excellent reconstruction materials. The National Archives Learning Curve site has a dedicated exhibition on Tudor Hackney

WEBSITE

(http://learningcurve.pro.gov.uk/tudorhackney/index.asp). As with the previous reconstructions, this virtual reality village has plenty of visual appeal but it is also based on solid historical and archaeological research. The contents of several of the houses are actually listed in some of the inventories and other documents which accompany the site. In addition to all of this rich material there is the story of the Daniells family and how they fell foul of Queen Elizabeth I. Their story can be studied from original sources, from an authored narrative or through a reconstruction drama, again based closely on the original sources.

Fig 5.10   Scenes from the Tudor Hackney resource on the Learning Curve

The main point with all of these reconstructions is that it is hard to see how else they could be made available to students other than through the internet. They also offer exciting opportunities for students to study historical interpretations in a meaningful way. For each interpretation, most students would enjoy investigating one or more of the following issues:

➡ How do we know how authentic the reconstructions are?

➡ How did the authors of each reconstruction make use of original evidence?

➡ What did the authors do when they had to reconstruct a part of the site for which evidence was limited or non-existent?

➡ What sites are near to me that could be reconstructed this way? What evidence would I need to give the web developers to create the reconstruction?

This final question has tremendous potential for engaging students and getting them using local records from the sort of sources outlined in the local history section above. It may also be an opportunity to devise an assignment for a vocational GCSE project in ICT or leisure and tourism. This issue is currently being explored as part of the GCSE history hybrid being developed by the Qualifications and Curriculum Authority.

Academic interpretations

Of course, it would be quite wrong to ignore the potential of the internet for written interpretations of history as well. The internet is increasingly becoming the key means of communication, publication and debate between academic historians. The rising popularity of relatively highbrow popular television programmes on a range of historical topics means that the general public and our students should also have access to the views of these historians on websites that support these programmes. This is increasingly common practice with factual programming.

WEBSITE

If you are interested in very high level and up-to-date academic thinking on historical topics then an excellent site is H-Net (http://www.h-net.org/). This might be more accurately described as a linked collection of websites in which academics in a wide range of humanities fields discuss issues and exchange ideas in an email discussion forum. H-Net is divided into specialist fields such as H-Albion for British and Irish history, H-German for German history and so on. It is only open to academic historians working in universities but this is not really a problem. The most valuable aspect of the site is the ability to eavesdrop on the exchanges of those who are best read and most up to date on current historical debates. A similar role is fulfilled by the website of the

WEBSITE

Institute for Historical Research (http://www.history.ac.uk). Particularly valuable are the discussions on newly published books, especially when the moderator of the discussions rounds up discussions with a summary of edited highlights. This is a very time efficient way for teachers to keep up to date with the latest research, and a powerful challenge to able students at AS/A2 level.

A more accessible forum for the views of academic historians is the History Heads resource which is part of Channel 4's web presence

WEBSITE

(http://www.channel4.com/history/microsites/H/history/heads/index.html).

This is an interesting but slightly eccentric collection of the views of historians on a range of issues and subjects, usually emanating from history television programmes produced by Channel 4. It is organized under a number of key headings:

➡ Opinion: Historians and others with firm points of view get on their soapboxes.

➡ Footnotes: Fascinating historical sidelights on a cornucopia of subjects and epochs.

➡ Out-takes: An exclusive look at everything historians said while the cameras rolled.

➡ Past imperfect: Hollywood or history? Fact and fiction on the silver screen.

➡ The library: Hefty extracts from newly published history books.

➡ Ask the experts: Historians put on the spot.

WEBSITE

Another excellent source of interpretations is the BBC's main history website (http://www.bbc.co.uk/history). As a general rule, the BBC commission top-notch academic historians to write accessible summaries of the latest thinking on popular academic areas. Thus Professor Ronald Hutton can be found writing about the Tudors and Professors Gary Sheffield and Richard Holmes about the Great War. Many of the flagship BBC television history series are also supported at the media zone area. For instance, you can recall sections of Simon Schama's *History of Britain*, such as the transformation of a modern church back to its pre-Reformation decoration

WEBSITE

(http://www.bbc.co.uk/history/multimedia_zone/audio_video/).

Other interpretations

The internet is also home to much less respectable and less studious interpretations than those listed above. Some of these are simply poor quality websites or websites with flaws, which can be used as the basis of an activity to improve it, as described earlier in this chapter. Other sites can be more accurately described as historical interpretations, even if they are not academic interpretations.

These different types of interpretations were very helpfully identified in 1993 by Tony McAleavy and his ideas still inform much of the current thinking about interpretations (see below).

Types of Interpretation	Examples
Academic	Books and journals by professional historians Excavation reports Lectures
Educational	Textbooks Museums Television documentaries Artists' interpretations
Fictional	Novels Feature films Television dramas Plays
Popular	Folk wisdom about the past Theme parks Nostalgic depictions in advertising
Personal	Personal reflection

The internet is noticeably absent from this list, mainly because it was very much less of a presence in the lives of young people in 1993 than it is today. Today, young people can easily access information on sensitive issues relating to present-day problems which purports to give a historical perspective but which may actually provide a rather one-sided or distorted view. Some of the worst culprits are time lines. Students are on the whole worryingly uncritical of the information found in websites and they tend to see time lines as 'value free'. Time lines such as these show that by carefully selecting the events you choose to enter into a time line, or the way you describe these events, you can easily make a time line anything but value free.

➡ Click on the section 'History of Israel' and then 'Historical overview'.

➡ Click on 'By Topic directory' under the heading 'EI Extra' and then 'Key Historical Events'.

➡ Click on 'The Party' and then 'History'.

➡ Click on 'about us' and then 'Our history'.

In his 1993 article, McAleavy made a range of suggestions for making use of different types of interpretations.

➡ Which parts of the interpretation are factual and which are points of view?

➡ How far are these views supported by evidence? How selective has the use of evidence been?

➡ What was the purpose and intended audience of the interpretation?

➡ How plausible is the interpretation?

➡ How far was the interpretation affected by the background of its author?

These suggestions were not written with websites in mind. However, they would work admirably with the time lines listed above and other time lines of a similar nature. They could also be used with other forms of popular interpretations such as:

WEBSITE

➡ Boston Globe on Gorbachev: (http://www.boston.com/globe/search/stories/nobel/1991/1991ai.html) This is an article celebrating the role of Mikhail Gorbachev as leader of the USSR. Its laudatory tone is in marked contrast to the attitude towards Gorbachev in Russia.

WEBSITE

➡ Irish Northern Aid Committee: (http://inac.org/) This is the website of an American organization which is closely linked to extreme Irish Republican groups and is regularly accused of raising funds for the IRA.

WEBSITE

➡ Remembering Bloody Sunday: (http://larkspirit.com/bloodysunday/) This site looks at the events of Bloody Sunday from the perspective of the marchers attacked by British troops.

WEBSITE

➡ Why I hate Ho Chi Minh: (http://www.ocweekly.com/ink/archives/99/24lede2-nguyen.shtml) A bitter attack on the Vietcong leader and his role in the Vietnam War.

WEBSITE

➡ The real truth about Martin Luther King Jnr: (http://www.martinlutherking.org/thebeast.html) This extreme site is a bitter attack on the civil rights leader, levelling a range of accusations. It is very strong stuff and must be viewed by teachers before any kind of use with students. You may want to copy extracts from the site to show students.

WEBSITE

➡ The Truth At Last: (http://www.stormfront.org/truth_at_last/index2.htm) This is an extreme right wing site. Like the previous site, it needs careful previewing before mentioning to students. That said, it is a classic example of how academic research can be selectively quoted and misrepresented to argue a cause, in this instance the cause being Holocaust denial. An excellent article on how sites such as this have misled students can be found at Teaching Zack to Think (www.anovember.com/articles/zack.html).

WEBSITE

▌Using the internet to exchange ideas

It is sometimes easy to forget that the 'C' in ICT stands for communication. The internet is a wonderful tool for communicating ideas and perspectives and exchanging ideas, questions and answers. Students from different schools who would probably never meet can use the internet to compare their views on important historical issues. Teachers can also exchange ideas about ICT and non-ICT issues. Such activities fit extremely well with the process of building collaborative learning communities, which many schools are trying to achieve and which forms such a key part of programmes such as the Critical Skills Programme.

Fig 5.11 **Extract from a student email conference involving schools and colleges, which was designed to help students during the revision period of their examinations. This discussion appeared on the commercial subscription service History Online**

WEBSITE

http://www.historyonline.co.uk

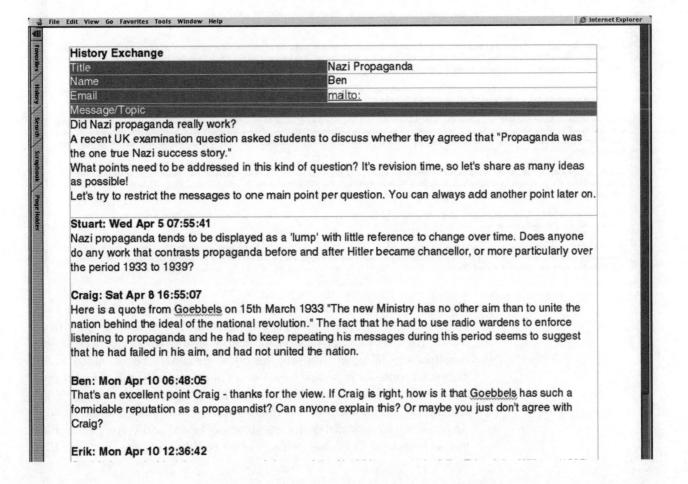

Figure 5.11 shows a small part of an exchange of views on propaganda in Nazi Germany. It was set up as part of a revision programme to keep students talking and thinking about their work during the Easter holidays and hopefully to aid revision! The students were from different history sets within the same college but there are also some contributions from teachers and academics from other parts of Britain, and also from Norway. Some schools and colleges have used email discussions to establish contacts between academic historians and their older students. Academic historians then set the key areas of debate and act as referees for the discussions that follow. This type of work, however, is in no way confined to older students. Figure 5.12 shows an extract from a story contributed by English and Irish primary school students to the Viking Network. This site encourages students from any part of the world to contribute their stories, articles, research findings, reports on site visits or anything else of interest to Viking historians.

Fig 5.12   **Extract from a story on the Viking Network**

WEBSITE   http://www.ncte.ie/viking/sto2.htm

File Edit View Go Favorites Tools Window Help   Internet Explorer

VIKING NETWORK IRELAND

THE VIKINGS ARE COMING!

A Viking Story Written by:

St. MICHAEL'S BNS, TRIM, CO. MEATH.

AND

BRAMPTON JUNIOR SCHOOL, CAMBRIDGESHIRE, ENGLAND

I was on the hill behind the village minding my father's sheep. I could see the small village to the south. The market was full of people. Beyond the village I could see the tower which had just been built in the monastery. This tower had been built because we had heard about the vikings. They had attacked and destroyed a village and monastery to the north. In this tower we could store our valuables and the people could shelter.

There was a strong wind blowing from the north and I watched the waves dash against the rocks. Far out at sea I could see a tiny object. At first I thought it was one of our fishing boats returning but as it came closer I could see a brightly coloured sail. It was a viking ship!

There was no time to lose. I must leave the sheep and warn the villagers that the Vikings are coming. To all the farmers I met I shouted, "The Vikings are coming!". They ran with me to the village. In the village people began to panic. Mothers ran to collect babies and small children. Mothers and wives hugged loved ones and promised to pray for them. Children and the old were crying. My mother told me to be brave and gave me her necklace for good luck. Then all the mothers and children and elderly hurried to the tower for safety.

Fathers and sons picked up the weapons. We had made wooden shields, axes, spears, knives and swords. I had a wooden shield and a knife. Our leader shouted, "Victory to the Saxons. Down with the Vikings!", and we set off to the beach to fight with the Vikings. The Viking ship was closer to the shore now. We could hear their blood-curdling cries and shouts. The coastline was rocky and the sea rough with the wind blowing. Perhaps the weather was on our side.

The Vikings were swimming to the shore to start fighting with us. I was fighting with a Viking. He was very strong and fierce. When the Viking turned around because someone called him, I stabbed him in the heart with my knife.

Our village fought bravely and long; many Saxons died, but more of our men waited on the beach in case any Vikings came out of the sea. The Vikings clothes were heavy because of the sea water and we could lift our swords and axes higher and quicker than the Vikings. The sea was red with spilt Vikings and Saxons blood. The noise of swords clashing and cries of pain had stopped. The Vikings who were not killed had swum back to their ship. We had won, but what would happen next time?

Many primary schools have made excellent use of email and also live video conferencing to exchange views and ideas with students in other parts of the world. The one word of caution for history in this respect concerns video conferencing. In many respects, historical debate is better suited to the thoughtful pause for reflection which email offers rather than live responses on a video conference. However, this is not a hard and fast rule. In April 2003, students on Merseyside used the video conference technology at the National Archives to interview two of the few surviving First World War veterans about their experiences. Of course, video or email conferencing does not need to be so exotic. Teachers in Bradford have developed a neat line in hypothetical historical situations in which students from different schools advise each other on important historical issues. Figure 5.13 shows an example of one exchange centring on the issue of appeasement in the 1930s. In this particular example students in one country represented the British position in the 1930s and the other school represented the German position. A fuller description of this activity and its impact is available on the National Curriculum in Action site (http://www.ncaction.org.uk/subjects/history/ict-lrn.htm). Clearly, careful teacher supervision is needed in an activity such as this to avoid silly answers, or the arrival of anachronistic statements not in keeping with the 1930s or informed by later knowledge. That said, such monitoring would be needed in any lesson. Indeed, activities such as this might well make teachers aware of anachronistic thinking in students that might not otherwise see the light of day.

WEBSITE

Fig 5.13 **An extract of the exchanges between the students in the email discussion on interwar Europe**

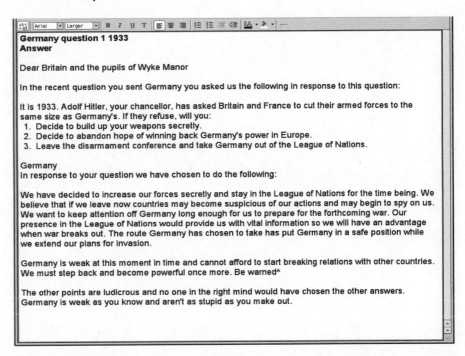

A final example, and a very valuable one, of email exchanges is the range of ideas and information that can be exchanged by teaching colleagues. Networks of academic historians were referred to earlier, but there are also growing networks of history educators. The Open University and other PGCE courses operate email networks in which trainee teachers share ideas on teaching practice. One of the most stimulating reads to be had on the internet is the exchanges contained in the History Teachers' Discussion Forum (http://www.schoolhistory.co.uk/forum/). Here teachers exchange news and information about forthcoming television programmes, useful websites, and interesting software and hardware. Above all, it is a supportive community of teachers who freely and generously share advice and ideas on all aspects of teaching history, whether it involves the use of ICT or not. For primary teachers one of a number of sites that exchange resources for history topics is Primary Resources History (http://www.primaryresources.co.uk/history/history.htm). This type of use is perhaps the ideal final example for this section, since it is indisputably an example in which the use of the internet adds real value to the teaching of history.

WEBSITE

WEBSITE

Chapter 6

Interactivity and authoring: Joined up history and ICT

In this section you will discover:

- The term interactivity is much used and much abused in connection with electronic resources. Genuine interactivity involves students in dialogue and in the transformation of knowledge, rather than the recall and transfer of information.

- ICT tools provide the opportunity for students to author products which demonstrate their understanding. This allows a range of different learners with different learning styles to show their understanding through media which best suit them.

- There are many authoring tools that can enhance students' enjoyment of history and their learning of it. These include word processors, presentation packages and a range of specialist software for authoring web pages, creating mind maps and so on.

What do we mean by interactivity?

Interactivity is a term often used in relation to electronic resources, but is it always used appropriately? All too often the term interactive refers to a resource which is little more than a multiple choice quiz. Such resources have their place in the teaching and learning process, and I have highlighted good examples, such as those on http://www.schoolhistory.co.uk (see chapter 1, page 18). That said, the place of such resources is pretty limited. They are good as ice-breakers to kick off a lesson, or for an informal pause in the middle of a session. However, they purely test knowledge alone and do little to develop understanding or powers of communication. To be fair to the providers of many such resources, teachers who use them are aware of the limitations. They make use of them exactly as they should be used. However, in too many cases these resources are promoted as genuinely interactive and presented to teachers as valuable learning experiences. I will not single out the worst cases but the type of resource is not hard to find. Some concentrate on aspects of content that, at best, can be described as peripheral – *Can you dress the Tudor jester in the right clothes?* Some are little more than games of chance – *Build your own pyramid and see if it stands up* – or of random selections where the key skill is the ability

WEBSITE

to click rapidly and repetitively – *Can you choose the right food for the wartime shopping basket?*

The essential problem with these types of resources is that for all the claims of interactivity they are, to all intents and purposes, passive. There is little or no opportunity for students to transform knowledge from one form to another, which is where most effective learning usually takes place. All the up-to-date research on effective learning, whether it be part of Critical Skills Programmes or accelerated learning approaches, show that students need to be active and to transform knowledge if their learning is to be memorable.

Many teachers, primary and secondary, who have looked long and hard at how ICT might be used to transform learning have recognized that quick fix software applications generally do not achieve this, and never achieve transformation unless they are part of a wider learning package. Most would agree that a more rewarding form of interactivity can be achieved using ICT. This is where ICT does not attempt to be the learning tool but where ICT supports the students as they transform knowledge. The role of ICT in this process is to provide access to relevant and useful information. It is also to provide students with tools which allow them to search, sort, select and present information from a range of data sources and create a new product from the selected information. In short, students will be authoring. In the process they will be transforming knowledge, which is surely a valid interpretation of the term interactivity. Furthermore, in a typical authoring activity students are likely to interact regularly with other students and with their teachers.

▌ What does authoring mean?

As with the term learning package in chapter 2, I have no wish to invest the term authoring with any special significance. It simply refers to activities and processes in which students create an end product. It is perfectly valid for a lesson or series of lessons to result in a discussion or a paper product. However, since this is a book about the use of ICT in history, the focus of this chapter is naturally on how students might use electronic resources to create electronic products! A number of examples of student authoring have already been described in chapters 1–5 of this book.

➡ In chapter 2, the example of a learning package based around Furness Abbey in Cumbria was designed with a final product in mind – a web based resource that the students would create (see figure 6.3b below on Furness Abbey and the learning package in chapter 2 on page 37).

➡ In chapter 3, the word processor was used in a variety of examples that involved student authoring of some description. This included: a piece of balanced writing on the Vikings; the transformation of statements on William the lord and William the villein from a jumbled list into a piece of writing; the annotation of the document on the Liverpool to Manchester Railway; and the table structure on Nazi youth policies.

➡ In chapter 4, students were drawing graphs and writing reports from data. They were also creating data files for themselves, as well as using the British Pathe catalogue to plan an opening sequence for a documentary television series.

➡ In chapter 5, student authoring took the form of reworking a website, writing reviews of sites, creating part of a publication on the Great War and publishing and exchanging their ideas across email conferences and websites.

All of these constitute examples of student authoring. In the context of this chapter, therefore, authoring means taking information in electronic forms and analysing, interpreting or transforming it in some way and then communicating the resulting understanding in some electronic form. This may or not constitute a more helpful definition of the term interactivity in the educational context. It is certainly more the kind of interactivity which we want on a routine basis in our classrooms. The interactivity in authoring is between student and student and student and teacher. It is also between student and different sources of information and computer applications. The ideal authoring task is one which might involve students using a range of applications – perhaps generating a hypothesis from a data file, checking this against a range of other sources on a range of websites and then presenting balanced conclusions in a presentation. In the rest of this chapter, the aim is to explore further examples of such approaches and the tools available to help students and teachers create their own masterpieces.

Authoring history: The word processor

The most obvious and widely used tool for student authoring is, of course, the word processor. Its properties and possibilities in terms of helping students with thinking and writing have already been explored in chapter 2. However, it is worth remembering that the word processor is an extremely flexible tool. In general terms, powerful word processors like Microsoft Word can handle images as well as text. They can also import data from spreadsheets. This makes the word processor a powerful tool for creating documents which incorporate a range of different types of data and media.

Hyperlinks
One of the most useful features for the teacher can be the hyperlink. This is a facility that means when a document is read on the computer (as opposed to a printout), a part of the text can be linked to another part of the text or to another document. When clicked, the hyperlink opens the document. The most obvious instance of its value is in creating a list of recommended websites for students to look at, as in figure 6.1a.

Fig 6.1 a   **List of recommended websites on the Gunpowder Plot of 1605**

WEBSITE

Gunpowder Plot Society
http://www.gunpowder-plot.org/
Detailed and imaginative site that explores all the conceivable possible angles of this event.

WEBSITE

Biography of Robert Catesby
http://www.gunpowder-plot.org/people/rcatesby.htm
Highly detailed biography of Catesby with detailed genealogical links making it very easy to trace all his relatives!

WEBSITE

Harvington Hall
http://www.harvingtonhall.com
Website relating to this historic building. The section on priest holes is especially relevant and interesting to students tackling this question.

WEBSITE

Tudor history
http://www.tudorhistory.org/
Interesting and lively site focused on Tudor history but with a range of different angles and approaches ranging from high level original sources to Tudor movies.

WEBSITE

Tudor biographies
http://www.spartacus.schoolnet.co.uk/Tudors.htm
Part of the excellent Spartacus website, this resource contains helpful summaries of key figures and some less well-known ones as well.

Fig 6.1 b   **Address bar (highlighted) of the website on Robert Catesby**

WEBSITE

http://www.gunpowder-plot.org
Click on 'The People', 'Personal Profiles and then select 'Robert Catesby' from the list of Principal Conspirators.

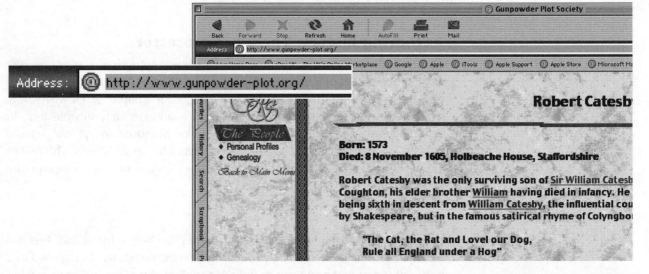

In this instance, the hyperlinks were created by simply copying the address of each website from the address bar of the browser page and then pasting this into the word processor file. A press of the space bar or the return button and the address becomes a live hyperlink. The other way to insert a hyperlink (for example, to another word processor file) is via the 'Insert' command on the menu bar. The 'Hyperlink' option can usually be found at the foot of the list.

Tackling Encarta syndrome

Technology today is becoming increasingly integrated, particularly via the internet. This can provide another useful device for the use of the word processor. In chapter 2, I mentioned the potential problem of Encarta syndrome (see pages 27–28). In this syndrome students simply located a source of information (often the Microsoft multimedia encyclopedia or perhaps a website) and printed it. They then pass off the work as their own not even attempting to conceal their actions, as they see nothing wrong with this approach. It is hard to say which of the two crimes is worse.

The word processor is an excellent tool to help tackle Encarta syndrome. Of course the first thing we must ensure is that we have set the task in the right way. Faced with an instruction such as 'Find out about Henry VIII' we all know what will happen. However, if students are asked to use the article to decide what five things everyone should know about Henry VIII, then we immediately have greater focus and we also have the option to customize the task to different levels of age and ability. We could set parameters such as:

➡ Being more specific about the audience, for example, what should KS2, 3 or 4 students know about Henry VIII and why the difference?

➡ Extending the list for A level students

➡ Limiting the five things to a specific time period

➡ Limiting to a specific theme (for example, early years, wives, break with Rome)

➡ Limiting to a specific section of the CD-ROM article or website.

Students can be taught to switch between Encarta and a word processor file easily. In the context of their enquiry they can then read the information source, copy items of relevance and transfer them to their word processor file. Once the material is transferred they can tidy it up appropriately. The word processor can count the number of words in a file in seconds, so in order to add additional rigour teachers could insist on a word limit for the final piece of work.

It is worth noting that this process is applicable to virtually any important figure, using virtually any high quality resources, whether it be a CD-ROM encyclopedia or a website. Finally, remember that good word processors handle visual images as well. This ties in to the wider agenda of not only using ICT but how the use of ICT helps us to meet the VAK challenge of providing inputs and outputs which use a range of different learning styles. A student who prefers to organize thoughts visually may prefer to present five key points as a series of points, arranged tastefully around a portrait of Henry VIII, as shown in figure 6.2. This was done using text boxes, which are explored in a little more detail in the section on presentation tools.

Fig 6.2   **Annotated portrait of Henry VIII using a portrait from the British Library**

Married six times

Broke with Rome in 1536

Word processor and web

Another potential benefit of the word processor's integration with web technology is the ability to edit web pages. For most schools the default web page browser is Microsoft Internet Explorer and the main word processor is

Microsoft Word. Using either the 'File – Edit with Word' command or the edit button on the toolbar of the browser, teachers or students can open a web page in Word and then change the page as they wish. This would be a very handy facility for an activity such as the web page on women in Nazi Germany on page 85, or the suggested task in which students add material to the BBC websites on the Vikings and/or Tudors. The revised page has to be saved on the local computer of course, as it is not possible to change a website which is on the web!

Fig 6.3a   **The 'Edit with Word' facility in the Internet Explorer browser**

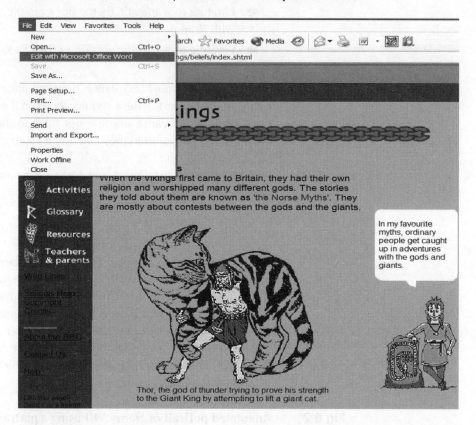

Authoring history: The desktop publishing package

Desktop publishing (DTP) software is almost as obvious a choice for student authoring as word processing software. There are many different packages to choose from ranging from the powerful commercial tools widely used in the publishing industry to relatively simple tools aimed at young primary students such as Textease (http://www.softease.com/textease.htm).

WEBSITE

The big advantage which DTP software has over word processing software is the focus on layout and also the greater facility for using graphics and other visual devices. Probably the most widely used example of the DTP package is the creation of a newspaper dated to a particular time. This task can be, and indeed has been, widely misused in the past. All too often it has been little more than a writing up exercise based on work in previous classes. As with every other use of ICT, it is important that the decision to use DTP software is based on the ways in which it can contribute to the students' enjoyment and understanding of the task and add an element of challenge or support not easily available without the use of ICT.

Thus, if students are using DTP software to create a newspaper article then it is important that the intellectual challenges specific to history in such an article are not forgotten. This means presenting students with limits and parameters, for example, giving them a brief that the article must be written from an unbiased point of view. It might well involve students working to a tight deadline, or being limited in the amount of space they can use. It will almost certainly involve the use of visual images, but should insist that those images are somehow tied to the text and not included purely for aesthetic effect. This might mean insisting on a reference to the image in the text and or insisting   that any images must have meaningful captions. The DTP package is an excellent tool for helping students to meet these challenges, but students will only address them if we as teachers set them in the first place! Good examples of the thoughtful use of DTP (and other) software can be found at the research database of Christchurch College, Canterbury

WEBSITE

(http://client.cant.ac.uk/research/case-studies/). Among many interesting examples is the case study of Blenheim primary school in Leeds, which used Textease to help students create a newspaper article about the Vikings. As it happens, this particular example was more focused on developing literacy skills than history skills, but the existence of clear aims and parameters comes through.

Authoring history: HTML tools

The terms authoring and HTML sound very technical but all it means is writing web pages. This is usually a stimulating activity as students are usually highly motivated by producing work for an audience. Remember that writing web pages does not necessarily mean that the pages written will be going on the web. Clearly the most exciting option is for students to carry out work that will be published on the world wide web which their friends and relatives, wherever they may be, will be able to view. On the other hand, most students are reasonable and realistic enough to recognize that this will not always be possible. To begin with, the combined work of an entire class or year group on just one project might well exceed the amount of space which a school has available for putting its materials online. Copyright is also likely to determine whether student authored web pages can be made available on the internet. Students will naturally get greater satisfaction working with a rich variety of media that includes original documents, paintings, photographs, cartoons, and sound and video clips. Creating web pages which include these items and which are for a school's internal use only will usually not be an infringement of copyright. However, if schools put student work containing such material on the web, then they will need to gain copyright permission. Most students are usually happy to create for an audience of their peers. Indeed, it is an additional and valuable learning experience for the above constraints to be explained to them.

Web authoring: Tools

So what about actually creating web pages? There are plenty of different tools out there for doing this. As already mentioned, powerful word processors like Word can open web pages and they can also save documents in web page (HTML) format. So can powerful desktop publishing packages such as Microsoft Publisher, Adobe PageMaker or QuarkXPress. Presentation software like Microsoft PowerPoint can also save presentations in HTML format. There are also, of course, specific software packages for authoring web pages, such as Microsoft's Front Page or Macromedia Dream Weaver.

Web authoring: Purpose

At this point, it is important to rein back and remember that our key purpose is enhancing the teaching and learning of history rather than training future web designers. With this in mind, it is probably fair to say that the simpler web authoring tools will probably meet the needs of the history classroom. If you are using the more complex web authoring tools then you may want to examine what, if any, aspects of progression in ICT are being tackled. This is not something to be dismissed lightly. If students begin to associate history with high levels of technology then it can only raise the status of the subject. Chapter 5 has also shown that for the history teacher the key, as always, is purpose.

For teachers, we have already seen one example of authoring with purpose – the list of links. Another is the PowerPoint presentation in HTML format. If schools have an intranet, it can be very useful to make a teacher presentation available for students to revisit or perhaps to study if they missed the original introduction to a topic. It is noticeable that many academics are now beginning to put lecture notes on their university websites for these reasons.

For students, the same core principles set out in chapter 5 for using web resources should be applied when students are creating web resources. It is simply not good enough for the aim of an enquiry to be to produce some web pages. This would not be acceptable if any other medium was in use, and ICT should be no exception. So, we need to be aware of why we as teachers might want to author for the web or why we want students to do so. These principles are being applied on a daily basis by teachers who are engaging their students in activities that involve a VAK approach and/or a commitment to working collaboratively. In the context of history, possible purposes for students to author web pages might be:

➡ To create resources for other students and schools: An obvious example here would be a student authored list of sites and/or reviews of sites relevant to a particular topic or issue.

➡ To create an improved version of a flawed site, or a different version of a web resource more suited to a particular audience: In this instance, KS3 students might take a KS3 resource and simplify it for KS2, or they might take a KS2 resource and upgrade it for use by KS3 students. KS2 students could do similar upgrading or downgrading.

➡ To communicate specialist knowledge: Web pages are an excellent way for students to demonstrate their understanding of particular areas such as: in-depth research on a particular theme; the nature of a historical debate on a particular issue; ways in which archaeological, literary or other evidence has been used or is being used to create new understandings about particular topics in history.

➡ To raise awareness of a local historic site or an aspect of local history: This could take the form of a formal historical report or it could be a website designed to attract visitors to a particular area or event such as a re-enactment. Figure 6.3b shows an example of the web resource which was constructed to generate interest in Furness Abbey in Cumbria. It was constructed using a web page template in a DTP package. Once the images and text were completed the software generated the actual web pages.

➡ To put a particular point of view: This might be to explore a particular historical event and present a conclusion. It could be to use a deliberate but meaningful anachronism by asking students to make web pages about a particular event in history, such as the arrival of the Romans in Britain or Henry VIII becoming head of the Church. These pages would naturally be in favour or opposed to these developments. Other types of pages might use current protest sites as a model to create the types of pages that might have been used by resistance groups in Nazi Germany or campaigners for better housing in Victorian cities.

➡ Communication and collaboration: Here students might take part in an email or video conference or they might contribute material to a site such as the Viking Network mentioned in chapter 5.

Fig 6.3b The front page of a website constructed by students working at Furness Abbey in Cumbria

CD–ROM Ch 6/Furness Abbey Student website Project

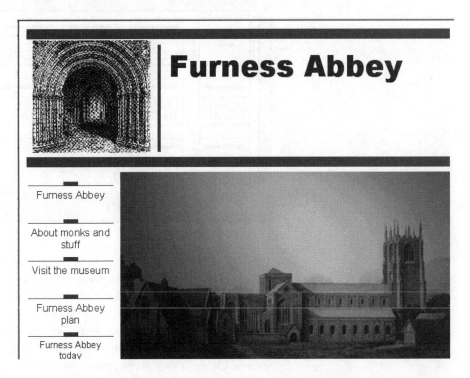

▍Authoring history: Presentation and multimedia tools

Presentation and multimedia tools usually work on the principle of separate slides or pages that are connected by hyperlinks. These hyperlinks might be as simple as a link to the next page. Alternatively, they might contain a different type of hyperlink such as a hot spot or button that causes some action to take place. There are many different multimedia authoring tools available. One of the most widely used is HyperStudio. Many students have created imaginative and inspiring multimedia presentations using Hyperstudio (http://www.hyperstudio.com). Some of the most exciting work has been in the London Borough of Hackney. The Highwire website in Hackney is well worth a visit to see what can and has been achieved (http://www.highwire.org.uk/). Hackney schools and others have featured regularly in the National Educational Multimedia Awards (http://www.bbc.co.uk/education/nema).

WEBSITE

WEBSITE

WEBSITE

Presentation software: PowerPoint for teachers

Even more widespread and more widely used than Hyperstudio is presentation software, particularly Microsoft's PowerPoint package. This really is a wonderful tool that many teachers have begun to explore and exploit to great effect in the classroom. Its most obvious use is for teaches to deliver presentations to classes, particularly to introduce topics and grab the attention of students. One of the greatest assets of PowerPoint is its ease of use combined with flexibility. One of the first features any user will notice is the range of different types of slide that can easily be created, as figure 6.4a shows.

Fig 6.4a   **Different types of slides offered by PowerPoint. The software actually offers more types than are shown here. It also has a number of design templates which give options in terms of colour schemes, borders and so on**

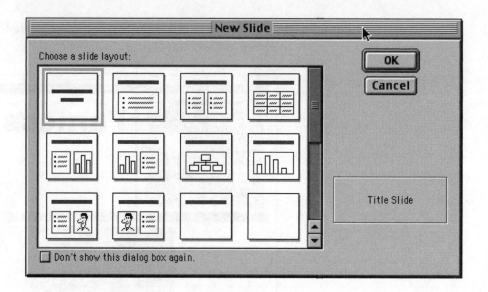

These different slide types neatly fit the needs of the history teacher. The most widely used is probably the slide with a title and bullet points. This is an immensely powerful tool for giving students a sense of the Big Picture, or connecting the learning in the terminology of the Accelerated Learning Cycle. PowerPoint is ideal for delivering key points of information and can be emphasized with animations and sound effects as they enter or leave the screen. Of the other slide types, the slide which has two columns of bullet points is very handy for emphasizing contrasts, such as causes and consequences, or changes over a period of time (one column showing 'before', the other showing 'after'). Graphs and other data can be imported directly from spreadsheet files. Images can be copied from CD-ROMs, websites or scanners and inserted into slides as well. A PowerPoint presentation consisting of a sequence of carefully chosen photographs can be an excellent way to prepare students for a field visit and/or follow it up.

PowerPoint also has the facility to insert and use hyperlinks in exactly the same way as word processors. Figure 6.4b shows an example of how this facility can be very useful. This presentation was used as an introduction to the study of appeasement in the 1930s. The enquiry made use of a range of different sources, including archive news film, original documents and a textbook. This presentation was used to pull together different elements from these sources into an introduction designed to grab the students' interest but also to get them to see how the different sources complemented each other in an historical enquiry. In this instance the PowerPoint presentation was an extremely useful tool for marshalling the material. Students had their own copies of the presentation, but the software really came into its own with the use of hyperlinks. The image on slide 2 was a hyperlink and when clicked the newsreel clip played. On slide 3, the cartoon was a hyperlink to the same image in a drawing package, which allowed it to be magnified and the final bullet point hyperlinked to the page from the Learning Curve website where the document was located together with a transcript and notes about the document.

Fig 6.4b   **A PowerPoint presentation using hyperlinks to model an enquiry for students**

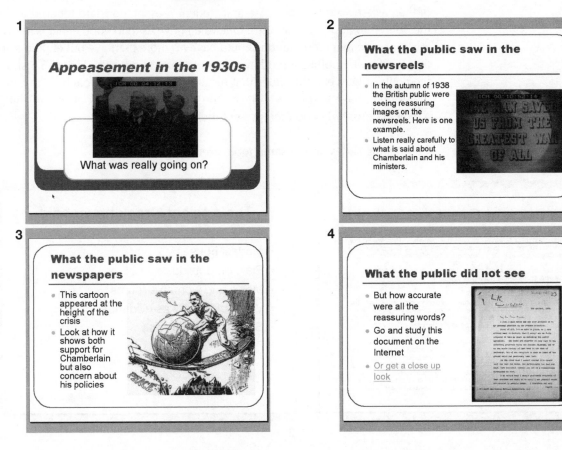

PowerPoint also has a series of useful tools for students who want to revisit a presentation or who missed it in the first place. The facility to save a presentation as an HTML file has already been mentioned. Another, even easier facility is to print the presentation. I have found the handout facility (figure 6.4c), which prints thumbnail images of slides along with a space for students to write notes, especially useful with older students.

Fig 6.4c   **'Handout' printing option in PowerPoint**

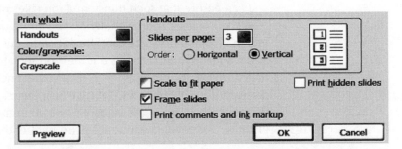

PowerPoint for students: Transforming knowledge

Students can use most of the PowerPoint features previously mentioned. Not surprisingly, however, they generally need a good deal of guidance and structure when asked to create a PowerPoint presentation.

One of the key elements of VAK learning is that students should demonstrate their understanding. It is hardly surprising that a common way in which they do this is through a presentation. However, presenting understanding effectively is a difficult skill. It needs careful modelling for students to understand what good practice looks like. If they do not get this guidance then all too often the result is a long, rambling presentation in which information is simply recounted rather than selected or shaped to a particular purpose. One of the easiest ways to make sure that student presentations are focused and to the point is to apply simple rules. One rule I have used to good effect is to insist that any slide in a presentation should have no more than five bullet points and that each bullet point should have no more than five words. Figure 6.5 shows the contrast between the slides that result from such an approach. In this task, the students have to use a website on the Ancient Greeks to look at daily life in a typical household and then present their findings.

Fig 6.5   **Contrasting slides on the same topic area**

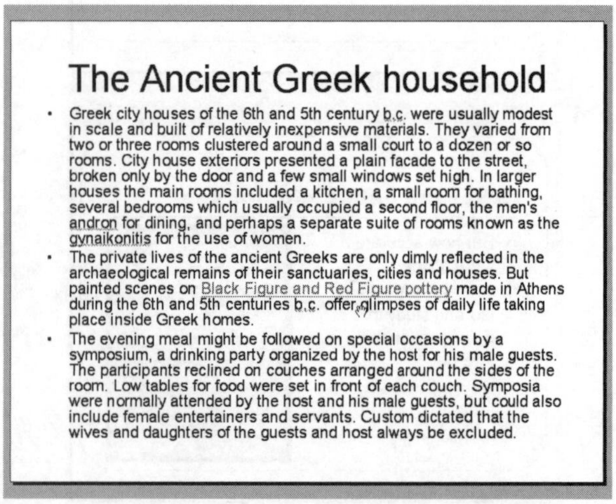

1

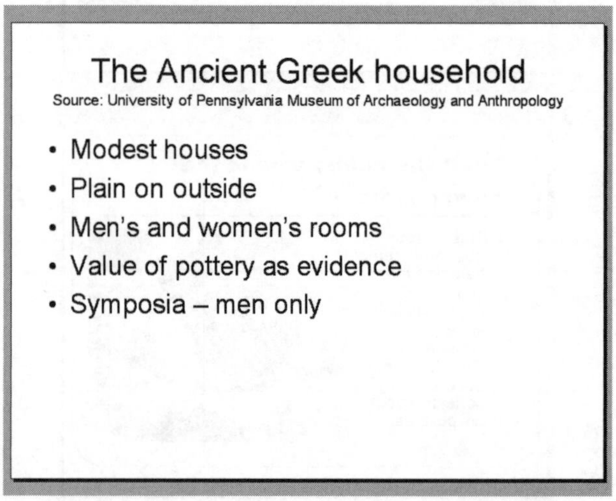

2

CD–ROM Ch 6/The Ancient Greek household PowerPoint presentation

At first sight it might appear that slide 1 is the more valuable piece of work as it contains more information. However, when we consider how the student might deliver this presentation it is clear it will simply be read out. As a result, students will develop few new skills in terms of presenting ideas. Just as importantly, slide 1 has actually been lifted wholesale from the site and simply pasted into the slide. This raises two important issues, the more important being that the information has not been read and certainly that the knowledge has not been transformed. By insisting that students create slides in the style of slide 2 you can ensure that such transformation takes place. In short, the student must read the original source material and must decide which of the points of information in this source carry the highest value and will therefore be included in the slide. When carrying out their presentation, students will be using the bullet points as prompts and should be encouraged to try and give the presentation without notes. Taking this approach is much more likely to embed the key knowledge in the student's long-term memory than the approach used in slide 1. A second important issue here is that at a very early age we can introduce students to the concept of plagiarism and how to avoid it. If young students in primary school can be made aware of this problem then we as history teachers are doing a great service to our colleagues in higher education! Of course, exactly the same principles apply as students progress through secondary school. One of the major causes of underachievement at GCSE level is the inability of students to marshal their considerable knowledge so that it meets the requirements of the question. In short, they bury the examiner in an avalanche of factual information without explaining how and why this information is relevant to the question being asked.

Admittedly, this is not an easy skill, which suggests all the more reason to try to get students working on it at an early stage. It's worth the investment because it's such an important skill not only in history, but also in life in general. Students at GCSE level might be asked to take exactly the same approach as shown in figure 6.5 to a particular section of their textbook. At AS/A2 level I have used the same techniques regularly. I have also used a variation on the same theme, which has turned out to be very popular. In this variation, students are given a presentation created by the teacher, such as figure 6.6. It is based on a particular source, such as an article from the A level history journal, *Modern History Review*. It is also very much in the style of slide 2 in figure 6.5. The task in this instance is that students have to make sense of this presentation. They have to read the article from which the presentation was created and then prepare to deliver the presentation themselves. They are free to amend the presentation if they do not like the way it has been summarized. In practice, of course, a whole class of students each doing a presentation can be time consuming and a little dull. An added element of interest can be introduced by randomly selecting students to present their thoughts on just one slide.

Fig 6.6   **A level presentation which students have to read around and present**

CD–ROM Ch 6/Nazis and Workers
PowerPoint presentation

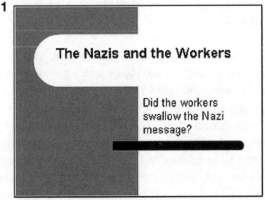

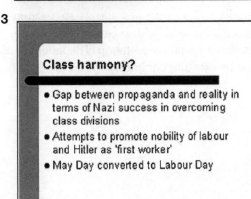

PowerPoint for students: analysing visual sources

PowerPoint is primarily a presentation tool, but it also has its uses as a tool to help students analyse source material. This is particularly true of visual sources. All too often, visual sources are seen as a panacea for students who struggle with text based material. VAK approaches have certainly shown that for some learners a visual input delivers more than a text based or oral input. However, visual historical sources are a slightly special case. A visual learner may well identify elements of a visual source, which other types of learner may not. Even here, however, there is no guarantee that the student will be able to see the significance of the small details in terms of explaining the importance, message or significance of the bigger picture. Closely connected to this problem is the difficulty many students have in stating succinctly exactly what that message or significance is. These difficulties are perfectly understandable. Most work students do in schools is not based around visual images. As a result, it is often very difficult to express views on a visual image in words. In history, this is a particular issue as many of the visual images are completely alien to students of the twenty-first century. Many images are from periods when literacy levels were very low or non-existent and so are intensely packed with information that a literate audience might not look for – never mind locate and interpret. Many images describe events and ideas that do not concern the modern young person – now or then.

PowerPoint cannot help students overcome these difficulties. They can only be overcome by good teaching. We as teachers need to teach our students the processes that historians and archaeologists use to interpret visual sources and also the ways they explain the meaning or importance of these sources. It is our responsibility to devise activities and enquiries which develop these skills in just the same way as we devise activities to help students develop an understanding of chronology, use of text sources, historical interpretations and so on. We also have to model for students the ways in which these understandings are encapsulated and communicated in words. What PowerPoint can do is to help teachers to help students by making it easy and enjoyable to analyse visual images.

Figure 6.7 shows an example in which students are asked to explain how and why a particular piece of evidence is useful. Faced with an image, such as that in slide 1, few primary school students will make much sense of it. Fortunately, it comes from the British Museum's children's COMPASS site on the Olympic Games and is accompanied by a commentary. The commentary explains that the image shows the long jump and points out a number of key features in the image that show how it is useful to historians. Where PowerPoint comes in is to provide the authoring environment, which allows students to break down the image and explain its value. In this particular instance, the teacher provides the main comment for the student. The student's job is to examine the commentary from the web page and add text boxes that turn the text commentary from the web page into a visual presentation. The labelling of the key features is done with the text box feature common to word processors and to PowerPoint.

Fig 6.7   **Analysis of a visual source using PowerPoint**

WEBSITE   http://www.thebritishmuseum.ac.uk/compass

Click on 'children's COMPASS/Tours/Sport in ancient Greece/familiar sports/long jumping' to locate the web page.

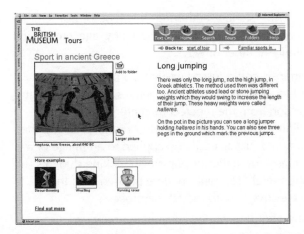

Students begin by looking at the web page. They study the image and the commentary and see how the image is useful to historians.

CD-ROM Ch 6/Olymic long jump PowerPoint presentation

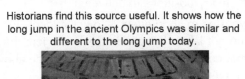

1

Students are then presented with a PowerPoint slide containing the image and the key statement, provided by the teacher. It is their job to support this statement by annotating the image. The key statement is the really critical element in the analysis. Whether this image is a Greek vase of the classical period or a political cartoon of the twentieth century, students need to be able to say what the value or the message of the image is and then support that key statement.

2

Students create text boxes. They are colour coded to show aspects of the long jump that are similar to and different from today. The key learning point here is that students are identifying the smaller elements of the picture, which come together to create the Big Picture. In the process they are generating snippets of evidence that can be used to support the key statement.

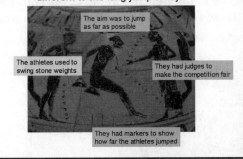

Historians find this source useful. It shows how the long jump in the ancient Olympics was similar and different to the long jump today. It shows that athletes in the ancient Olympics used weights so they could jump further. This does not happen today. On the other hand it shows that there were judges in the ancient Olympics. This does happen today.

Students are asked to turn their thoughts on this visual source from a mainly visual mode of expression to a text based form of expression. They are asked to select just two of the examples used in the presentation and to add suitable connecting phrases.

The final stage of this task is vital, particularly in the latter stages of history courses in secondary schools. The ability to explain *in writing* the message of a political cartoon, or to explain *in writing* whether a photograph presents a misleading view of a particular event is a key element of most assessments from Year 9 onwards.

Like so many examples involving student authoring, this type of task can be applied to almost any visual image, used with almost any age group and customized in an almost infinite number of ways.

➡ The image being examined could just as easily be a piece of Tudor propaganda praising Elizabeth I or attacking enemies of the Tudors. It could be a *Punch* cartoon from the nineteenth century criticizing Victorian social conditions or from the twentieth century attacking the European dictators. It could just as easily be applied to an image of a present day hero such as a footballer or pop singer. Asking students why the star in question might (or might not) be pleased with this image can be a very effective way to model the process.

➡ Different elements of scaffolding can be provided or removed. One variation of this example might give the students the key statement and the text boxes arranged to one side of the slide and the students simply asked to locate the right box in the right place. At the other end of the scale, the task could provide students with no text boxes and no key statement. There are clearly many positions in between!

➡ One further variation I have used to good effect is to get students to write text boxes that contain not labels but good questions. Here the teacher has the veto on what constitutes a good question. In the above example, a good question might be: 'What is the job of the man on the right?' Once a good question is asked the teacher answers it and the student can annotate appropriately.

PowerPoint for students: Reconstructing the past

A similar use of PowerPoint can be made to help students with an activity that I call 'plausible reconstruction'. In this scenario, students are given a reconstruction of a scene from their period of historical study, such as figure 6.8 below. They are then asked to suggest what the characters in the scene might be thinking or saying.

Fig 6.8   **Plausible reconstruction of a scene in the trenches in the Great War. Taken from *Essential GCSE Modern World History* published by Hodder Murray**

CD–ROM Ch6/ Trench Reconstruction
PowerPoint presentation

It is important to stress at this point the term plausible reconstruction. If this is not stressed then this activity could easily become little more than an exercise in imaginative fiction. This is not to denigrate imaginative fiction, but it has little place in the history class. This exercise does involve a certain amount of imagination, of course, but it is more one in which students engage emotionally with soldiers in the trenches. It is also a way in which text based work can be made more accessible to the visual and kinesthetic learner, especially if the kinesthetic learner can be allowed to act out their re-creation.

I have found this type of task most effective when used in conjunction with a collection of text sources from the time describing different aspects of life in the trenches. The role of the teacher is then to challenge students as they create their speech bubbles. The challenge that the students must meet is to show how and why their comments are plausible. For each thought or speech articulated, the teacher will be asking 'On what evidence are these comments based?'

As with the previous type of activity, this basic approach is applicable to almost any aspect of history. The scene from the trenches could be a scene from an Anglo-Saxon village, a Roman amphitheatre, an Aztec temple, a market in the Indus Valley, a medieval monastery, a Tudor court and a Victorian park. PowerPoint simply adds a dimension of interest and flexibility. The task could readily be replicated using paper, but using PowerPoint allows all the same advantages of ease of review and redrafting as the word processor. PowerPoint also has a wide range of speech bubble layouts (they are known as 'Callouts' and can be found in the 'Autoshapes' menu on the drawing toolbar). PowerPoint is also a multimedia authoring software tool and so some students might be more inspired by the prospect of using sound instead of, or as well as, their speech/thought bubbles. The sound could be a recording of the speech bubbles or could even be suitable background music. It is very easy to add sound to a PowerPoint slide using the 'Insert' menu and the 'Movies and Sounds' command.

PowerPoint for students: Analysing the moving image

As well as sound, PowerPoint is also able to handle video files. Few teachers will dispute the attraction that the moving image has for so many students. Moving image usually carries emotion and a sense of drama. Even so, there is always the danger that we do not get the full intellectual value from the vast archive of moving image resource that is available to us. This issue is explored in greater detail in chapter 7, but it's worth looking at a few examples of how students can make use of PowerPoint as an authoring tool that exploits the interest of moving image materials.

Figure 6.9 shows one way in which this can be done. In this example, students were asked to create a presentation about the media skills of Martin Luther King Jnr. As you would expect, they were required to support points they made by referring to evidence. The slight difference in this instance is that the supporting evidence was not the usual extract from a text source or a photograph or other image. What appears to be a photograph of King on the slide is in fact the first frame of a video clip. This was inserted into PowerPoint using the 'Insert – Movies and Sounds' command. When the image of Dr King is clicked it plays a short video clip. The key here is that the video is being used not as an interesting novelty but as a piece of evidence to support a viewpoint.

Fig 6.9   **PowerPoint slide from a presentation on Martin Luther King**

CD–ROM 🗁 Martin Luther King

Students can also use moving pictures in PowerPoint to create very simple television programmes. Technically, the process is very simple. Students insert the video clip and then insert and record a sound clip as described earlier in the example of the reconstruction drawing of the trenches. This tends to work more effectively with clips from earlier periods because they are generally silent. Students could well locate a silent clip showing Victorian transport, conditions in the trenches and evacuation in the Second World War, and then add their own commentaries to accompany these tracks. There are, however, some important limitations in using PowerPoint this way. Clips cannot be edited and the soundtrack and video clips have to be activated by a click of the mouse – they are not synchronized. This type of technology is examined in more detail in chapter 7.

Authoring history: Other authoring tools

PowerPoint is probably the most widely available and easily accessible authoring tool for most history teachers. However, it is worth looking at the wide range of other authoring tools which are available. Many are aimed at specific target audiences – age specific or subject specific – and not at history teaching. However, almost any product that involves students creating products and communicating their understanding is likely to be of interest to teachers looking to enhance the teaching and learning of history.

Chronology and time lines

Several companies publish software specifically designed to help students get to grips with chronology and show their understanding of the chronology of a particular issue, theme or period. It is sometimes easy for teachers to forget how much contextual knowledge they actually hold in their heads. Consequently, it is easy to forget how little contextual information some students hold. Thus, without the benefit of having studied the sequence of events, it is quite possible that many young students might not be aware that the Romans preceded the Saxons who preceded the Vikings. It is quite possible for students to have a firm notion that the Nazis were involved in the Great War. Equally, it's quite easy to see how a student might wrongly sequence some of the events leading up to the murder of Archbishop Becket. Figure 6.10 shows an example of a time line on this very issue designed to help students get the sequence of events clear. It was created using Chronicle, a piece of software developed by the Scottish Council for Educational Technology (now part of Learning and Teaching Scotland; http://www.itscotland.org.uk/). There are several other packages around for creating timelines like this. A good example is Softease Timeline (http://www.softease.com/timeline). Like most of these packages it is targeted at primary school history classes. However, there are plenty of occasions when secondary schools could make use of packages such as these. The majority do more than simply create time lines. Most have a facility to attach text, audio or video files to particular dates, making the time line a more multimedia experience. It also opens up the possibility of setting students a task in which they correctly match source extracts to particular dates, adding extra challenge beyond the aim of sequencing events in the correct order. In figure 6.10, the events of 1135 are connected to a text document on the troubles of King Stephen's reign and the events of 1170 are connected to a short video clip.

WEBSITE

WEBSITE

Fig 6.10   **Time line of events leading to the death of Thomas Becket, Archbishop of Canterbury. The small icons indicate those text and video files that will be launched when clicked**

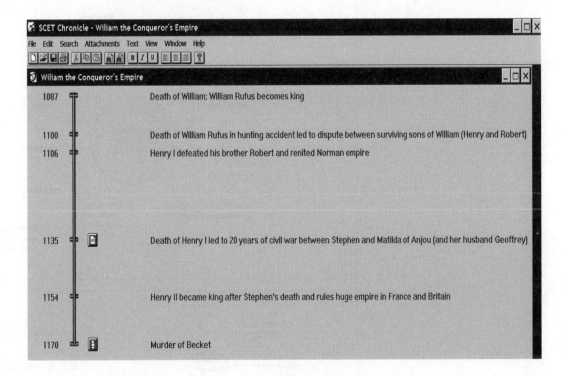

Recording and structuring knowledge and ideas: Mind mapping

Many teachers in primary and secondary schools have made excellent use of mind maps with students in a wide range of subjects. There are many publications which explore the virtues of this approach and which describe inspirational examples of its use. Mind maps are very useful tools for students in history. They can be used to brainstorm causes and consequences of events. They can be used to show change or contrast between two periods. They are very useful to learners who like to think visually or are kinesthetic learners in that they bring a visual and active dimension to the high level conceptual process of sorting and categorizing information. Mind maps can of course be drawn on paper, a whiteboard or overhead projector acetate. However, there are some neat software packages available designed to help teachers and students create their own mind maps. Figure 6.11 shows an example of a mind map that developed in two stages. First of all, students were asked simply to brainstorm anything they could remember about their recent work on Ancient Egypt. In the second stage, the mind mapping software was used to categorize these points and rearrange them into a mind map that was more conceptually structured. The random jumble of points was rearranged into a more ordered form that addressed the issue of why Egypt was powerful, taking it beyond the simple collection of data. Figure 6.12 shows the same software in use as figure 6.11 – Inspiration. Inspiration is an American resource (http://www.inspiration.com/home.cfm) but is available from a number of distributors in the UK. In this example, upper secondary students were investigating why the Weimar Republic government in Germany survived a series of crises in 1919–23 but failed to survive in 1933. The left hand diagram was a summary of a much more detailed mind map completed in earlier lessons. The task of the students was to examine the reasons for the failure of Weimar in 1933 and, in the process, consider how many factors had changed in the intervening ten years.

WEBSITE

Fig 6.11   **A mind map on the Ancient Egyptians**

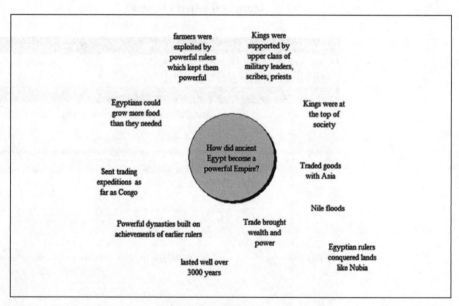

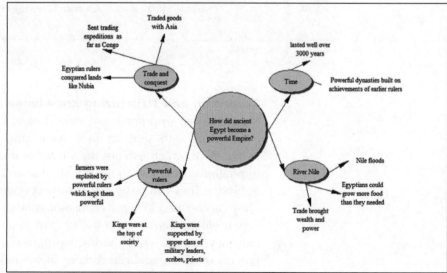

Fig 6.12   A mind map on the Weimar Republic

Local history and fieldwork history

The potential for the internet to support local history studies has already been set out in chapter 5 (see pages 96–98). Authoring software provides ideal opportunities for students to create presentations and products about their locality or the area they have investigated in a local study. An obvious vehicle for this is to create web pages on a particular site. Web authoring software exists for this purpose and has been explored above. However, one resource used in the south west of England to add an extra dimension to this is InfoMapper (http://www.webbased.co.uk/infomapper/). This resource is to all intents and purposes web authoring software. However, it structures the authoring process in such a way that web pages created using InfoMapper are navigated by geography – essentially clicking on an area of a map. Thus a series of web pages on a local area could be navigated by clicking on a map and gradually zooming in on the locality being studied. Of course this device need not be confined to British local history. It might well be used to examine the impact on America of Tudor explorations or the impact on central America of Aztec migrations. It could just as easily be used to conduct case studies of voting patterns in 1920s Germany or examine two different areas in the USA that were in favour of or opposed to the introduction of Prohibition.

WEBSITE

Panorama software

Another very handy tool for teachers in many different subjects is Panorama. This is a very simple type of authoring software that produces very satisfying results. Panoramas can be especially useful as preparation for a fieldwork visit or follow up to a fieldwork visit. It can also be very useful if you the teacher or just one or a few students have been to a historic site, perhaps on holiday. The panorama can give some sense of the geography of the place in question. Many historic sites have discovered the value of this tool for giving potential visitors a sense of what their site actually looks like. Figure 6.13 shows an example from the website of Romsey Abbey in Hampshire (http://www.romseyabbey.org.uk/panorama.htm). At first sight it looks like a still image, but a look at the controls shows you that this panorama file allows you to look around the abbey as though you were in the centre of it. It also allows you to zoom in on particular areas of interest or to get a better view of details, such as windows or statues.

WEBSITE

Fig 6.13   Panorama of Romsey Abbey in Hampshire (© Astarte Digital)

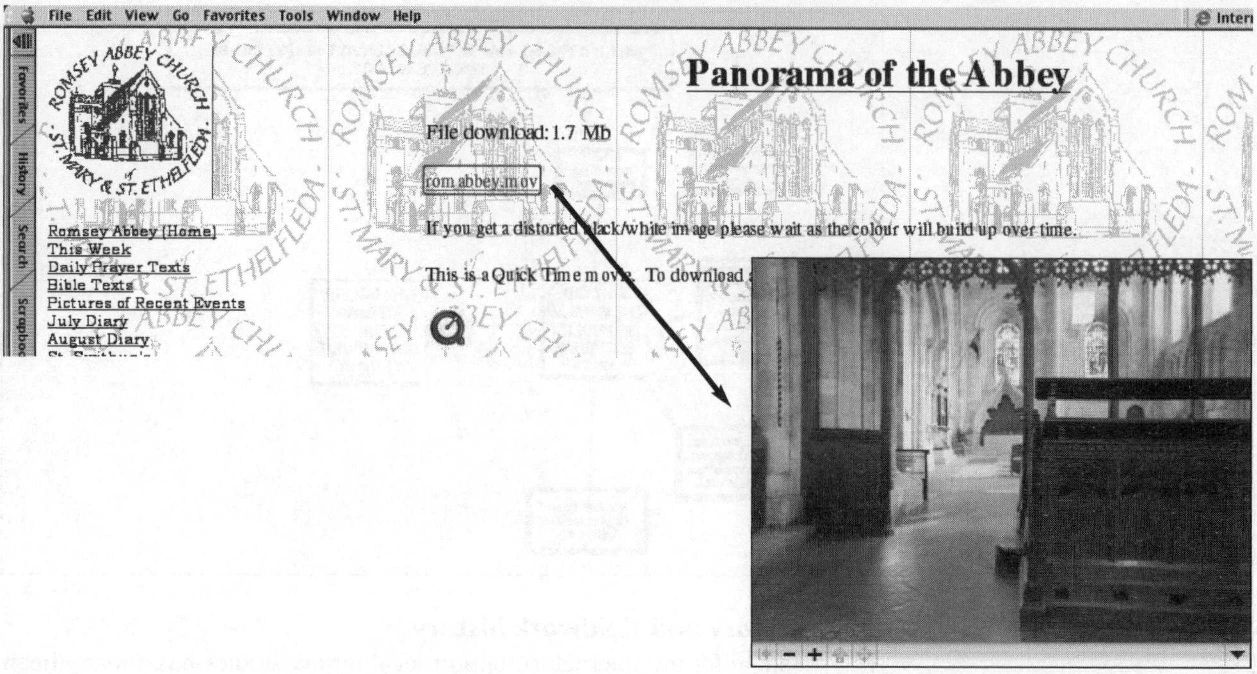

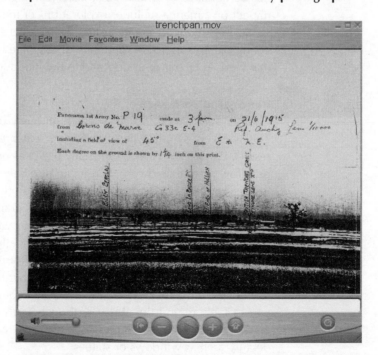

WEBSITE

The Channel 4 Time Team website (http://www.channel4.com/history/timeteam/index.html) also contains panorama files for many of the sites they have excavated in their various series. It is even possible to scan images of large documents and create panoramas of these. Figure 6.14 shows another image from a panorama created from a series of photographs designed to help artillery commanders in the Great War. The photographs were taken in sequence and designed to be spread out on a large table. This would involve some major practical difficulties in a classroom, so the ability to see the panorama of the trenches in this format could be both practical and powerful.

Fig 6.14   **A panorama created from Great War artillery photographs**

Creating these panoramas is very straightforward. What's more, the process of creating a panorama is a kinesthetic learner's idea of heaven! It involves moving around the relevant site. Better still it involves using a gadget – the digital camera. You need to generate the images in the first place, taking care to keep the camera as far as possible on a central axis (here a tripod is invaluable). There are many different software packages available to create these files, which are usually saved in standard formats that can be played on almost any computer. One of the best places to evaluate which software and/or hardware is best suited to your needs is panoguide.com (http://www.panoguide.com/). This site is dedicated to giving users all the available information about this type of resource.

WEBSITE

Creative virtual reality

A tool likely to become more common and more widely used is authoring software for virtual reality environments. At present, virtual reality is relatively expensive and difficult to create, and is the preserve of specialist organizations (see chapter 5). However, technology is constantly adapting and it may be possible in the not too distant future for schools to create virtual reality reconstructions of sites they are interested in. In the meantime, some schools are experimenting with resources like Creative Virtual Reality Picture Gallery (http://www.vr-education.com/education.htm). This resource was originally designed to help students in modern languages. However, its structure is ideal for getting students to think about historical sources and how they are presented and interpreted. In a nutshell, the resource allows the creation of virtual reality galleries which the user walks around and explores (see figure 6.13 and 6.14). These exhibits can be simply read or viewed by the user or they can be more interactive in that they can be linked to audio files, video files or websites. Many students would enjoy using such resources. However, they would get even more satisfaction from creating the resources themselves. As figure 6.15a and 6.15b shows, this is actually remarkably straightforward. A separate piece of authoring software gives students an aerial view of the gallery. Students select the gallery they are going to use. They then select each exhibit point; decide which source will be on that exhibit point; and whether it will be supported by links, commentaries and so on. This has huge potential in terms of motivation and the 'wow' factor of creating your own virtual resource. However, it also has great potential in terms of getting students to think. As long as certain parameters are established, the selection of source material, the accompanying commentaries, the positioning of different types of sources in relation to each other all raise important questions about how past events and people are interpreted and presented to the public in museums and galleries.

WEBSITE

Figures 6.16a and 6.16b show examples of tasks that would fit well with the Creative Virtual Reality Picture Gallery resource. However, the key in each resource is the element of selection. Students must decide on the relative importance and significance of each object and the extent to which it informs the viewer about the events under examination. If resources such as this engage students in the medium they are creating, but also get them thinking about how the presentation of their work will impact on their audience, then teachers interested in history, ICT, citizenship and a range of other skills will be very happy – a good example of joined up work with ICT!

Fig 6.15a An example of one of the galleries created using Virtual Reality Picture Gallery

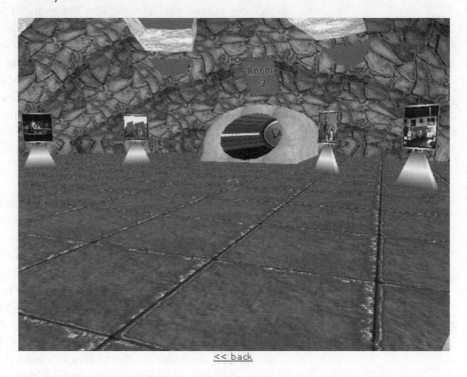

Fig 6.15b The authoring mechanism for the galleries. Students choose which gallery or galleries they will exhibit in. Then they select sources to be presented on each picture plinth

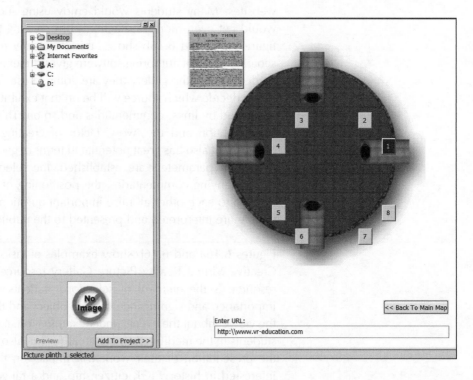

Fig 6.16a Activity about Ancient Egypt suited to the use of creative virtual reality

The British Museum needs your help! They want to put together an exhibition:

Ancient Egypt – an introduction

The trouble is, the experts in the British Museum know so much about Egypt they cannot decide what to put in or leave out of the exhibition.

This is where you come in.

➡ Work in pairs or small groups and come up with a list of all the possible objects, images and other sources that could go in the exhibition.

➡ Then decide which are the most important.

➡ You should then review your choices and make sure that at least some of them are attractive and interesting as well as important.

➡ If you have time, you could also come up with some quiz questions about Ancient Egypt. See if the rest of your class can answer them!

Fig 6.16b Activity about the Second World War suited to the use of creative virtual reality

A museum has come to you for help. They are having trouble deciding how to allocate space for their exhibition on the Second World War. Your job is to help them decide. They have 20 sources and room for 12 to be displayed. They want you to decide:

➡ how many themes there should be (for example, Battle of Britain)

➡ how many sources in each theme

➡ captions for each source.

Chapter 7

Digital video in the history classroom

In this section you will discover:

- Digital video makes a greater range of media available than ever before, in a form that makes it more practical to analyse and create new versions of the media than we have ever had before.

- As a resource, moving image is uniquely powerful in conveying a sense of place, period and drama. It connects powerfully with students' emotional intelligence.

- In a digital age, history can help students develop the media literacy needed to make them intelligent consumers of the media.

- History is particularly well served in terms of having access to a vast archive of news reportage and other clips from the twentieth century.

- Digital video has many qualities that can enhance the use of Hollywood movies in the analysis of historical interpretations.

- Digital video offers opportunities to engage students through whole-class teaching or individual work on moving images.

- Digital video resources allow the creation of students' own video packages – the ultimate multisensory and VAK experience!

History teachers have long used video in a variety of ways. They have played students the specially commissioned schools programmes produced by the public broadcasters. They have used mainstream television programmes to give students a deeper insight into particular issues, or simply to stimulate their interests. They have used extracts from feature films to give a sense of period, or perhaps to deconstruct a particular interpretation of an historical event. Video is the classic multimedia experience and can provide a valuable input for VAK learners, as well as engaging with the emotional side of history.

Why does digital video matter?

Engaging students

This begs the question of why history teachers should be interested at all in digital video as opposed to the traditional VHS tape form. There are several important reasons:

➡ The obvious one is the potential motivation of creating an interesting multimedia product, particularly one based on film.

➡ There is also the potential impact on your students' perceptions of history. Using digital video in history is likely to reinforce the relevance and value of history as a subject in the minds of your students, and may also shift some attitudes among colleagues as well!

➡ There is an obvious potential in work such as this for students to achieve high levels of attainment in ICT. Achieving this within a meaningful subject context is the holy grail for many ICT co-ordinators who, with the best will in the world, cannot be expected to have a detailed knowledge of the demands and complexities of history as a discipline. It is therefore incumbent on history teachers to at least meet the ICT colleagues halfway in this respect.

At the risk of stating the obvious, the potential of using digital video does not lie in the simple showing of film. Showing a documentary to the whole class will be no more or less engaging whether shown on VHS or through a digital projector. In fact, as a general rule, the showing of any lengthy film resource, such as a documentary of 30 minutes or more, is probably best shown on the traditional VHS and television combination.

Where digital video has real potential is in much more specific, targeted types of use. Digital video allows much greater control over video resources than we have ever had before. Storing video digitally (usually on computer) will allow you to select precisely the parts of video resources you want to use. For example, digital video makes it much easier than using VHS to store and show three to four short clips which present contrasting views of the same event. Digital video (with the right software) makes it realistically affordable and relatively easy to edit and reshape video resources. Digital video equipment also allows the user to remove, amend or completely re-record soundtracks. In the case of silent footage, you will be able to give soundtracks to clips which previously were either silent or had been given soundtracks by television programme makers. Digital video will also allow your students to become expert talking heads in their own presentations and documentaries. These opportunities are explored in greater detail later in this chapter.

Moving image/media literacy

Digital video also provides teachers with a huge potential to help students develop greater media literacy. It provides us with the resources and tools, which for the first time allow us to tackle moving image sources with the same rigour and imagination that we have been applying to text and still image sources for many years. In an age when young people increasingly use the television and internet as their main source of information it is important to help them develop a sense of critical awareness. The borders between television, internet and film are becoming increasingly blurred, and the distinctions between these different types of literacy are likely to become less meaningful.

History teachers are in an especially strong position to help students develop this type of media literacy. To begin with, since the introduction of the national curriculum, teaching and learning in history has developed a range of powerful strategies for dealing with print and still image media. Students in primary and secondary classrooms know that newspaper articles or propaganda posters contain valuable information and insights into contemporary values. They also know that such sources must be treated with caution if they are being used as factual records. Students know that extracts from contemporary literature are valuable, but are probably not to be used in the same way as secondary sources written many years after the events. Most students can interpret photographs, political cartoons or other visual images effectively.

Secondly, the history of the twentieth century is a key feature of primary and secondary school history. This is especially significant in terms of students developing their moving image literacy. The power of moving image and the media in general should not be underestimated. From the 1920s onwards, moving image steadily became the most important source of information about the world around us. The development of newsreel films, which accompanied entertainment features, was fundamentally important to the development of news media. Sometimes by accident and sometimes by design, moving image also became the most important source of misinformation in the twentieth century.

We have already seen one example in chapter 6 (see page 119) in which the presentation of the appeasement crisis of 1938 was in marked contrast with the behind the scenes documents and indeed with the public mood generally. This was a classic example of the media shaping the news as much as reporting it. This is not to suggest a dark conspiracy or the sinister hand of government censorship. In Britain, there was relatively little government censorship of moving image output in the First or Second World Wars or at any other time. Most research suggests that film makers censored themselves and conformed to the war effort. Most, in fact, went considerably further and voluntarily produced material to support the war effort and denigrate the enemy. The Walt Disney Corporation pulled few punches with its propaganda output during the Second World War. One of the most effective pieces of propaganda ever was the Donald Duck cartoon 'In Der Fuehrer's Face'. This and other Disney features can be found online (http://disneyshorts.toonzone.net/years/1943/derfuehrersface.html). While it is an interesting and amusing watch today, it is also a reminder of how something as seemingly innocent as Donald Duck (and of course all his other cartoon friends) can become an integral part of shaping a national attitude towards the war effort.

WEBSITE

So, it is important that students examine the provenance and purpose of moving image material. At the lowest level of ambition it may encourage students to think about the present day power of advertising, sponsorship and product association. More importantly, it should get them thinking about the relationship between the film maker and the audience. For example, it would make a good activity for students to compare the reportage of the First and Second World Wars with more recent conflicts. There would be similarities and differences as the political relationship between government and broadcasters changed. Just as interesting is the relationship between broadcasters and audiences. Paradoxically, it is arguable that some of the more graphic war scenes, such as those from Dunkirk in 1940 or the Somme in 1916, were rather less sanitized than most of the images shown from the Iraq conflict of 2003/4. This reflects a further paradox in which television news broadcasters were working outside government control (even though British forces were at war) but arguably imposed greater restrictions on their coverage in an attempt to conform to guidelines on taste and decency. These and many other issues would arise from newsreel and other moving image material broadcast in the USA in the twentieth century and, of course, in the Soviet bloc countries during the communist era.

So far we have only considered news reportage, but we should not forget the other types of moving image that students look at in the course of lessons and beyond. In the case of history television programmes, a common device is to show old footage with a commentary read out as the footage unfolds. It is worth remembering that these two sources did not originally belong together and they have been put together by the film maker to create a story of some sort. Students need to be aware of how a commentary can shape our reactions to and perceptions of a moving image. Finally, we should not forget the power of the Hollywood movie in shaping perceptions of the past (and often the present, by extension). A recent survey found that around 50 per cent of respondents believed that the Battle of the Bulge and the Hundred Years' War were fictional. Around 30 per cent thought the same thing about the Cold War. By contrast King Arthur was real in the minds of 57 per cent and even Conan the Barbarian came in at 5 per cent. Such surveys have a habit of revealing what their authors want to see, of course, but the existence of King Arthur in so many minds is surely connected to the prevalence of this story as a source for so many movies. Some 37 per cent of respondents felt that Kevin Costner's film about Robin Hood was an accurate depiction of events, and studies in the USA suggest similar acceptance of movies such as *Pearl Harbor*, *U-571* and *The Patriot* as fundamentally authentic records of past events. Our task is not so much to rubbish these accounts, but to make students aware that the priority of the film maker is not always historical authenticity – as generally this is too complex and gets in the way of the story.

WEBSITE

WEBSITE

WEBSITE

There are some excellent sources of material to help students and teachers explore the issue of moving image literacy. The British Film Institute (http://www.bfi.org.uk/education/) has a range of interesting material on its website and in its collection of published resources. It also runs training sessions for teachers. Their focus is primarily on film and media studies but there is much material of interest for teachers of history as well. This includes free downloadable resources, such as the excellent Moving Images in the Classroom (http://www.bfi.org.uk/education/resources/teaching/secondary/). Another organization which offers excellent support for teachers is Film Education (http://www.filmeducation.org/). This charity's whole raison d'être is to make it easier and more rewarding for teachers to use moving image in subject teaching. They have regular features on teaching issues which can emerge from current Hollywood releases. They also have a wide range of free and purchasable resources, including guides on writing film storyboards, summaries of films based on historical events and ideas on how to use films. Film Education also produces the *History In Motion* CD-ROMs that look at important historical events through film. They contain a large collection of clips, excellent contextual resources and a self-contained editing suite, which allows students to create their own documentaries on the events being studied.

▌ Where to find digital video resources

It seems fairly obvious that before we can exploit this new technology and achieve the lofty aims set out in the previous paragraphs, we need to know where we can get hold of digital video resources.

Ad hoc access to digital video: PC television and PVR

If you are a little bit technically minded, you may wish to consider PC television software. This involves a special card in your computer and specialist software. If you are buying a new computer this facility is sometimes provided as an option in the package you buy. Alternatively, you can purchase a Personal Video Recorder (PVR) that plugs into one of the ports of your computer. These options allow you to receive television programmes on your computer. You can also watch programmes from a VHS on your computer screen. You can save the programmes to your hard disk, take still shots from the programmes and with the right editing software create edited highlights. The great advantage of this is the ease of showing short clips from different sources. Many teachers use this technique to compare the portrayal of particular historical characters or events in movies from different periods. They may also compare this portrayal with portrayals in different factual programmes. Actual examples of this approach are explored later on pages 142–147. The big disadvantage is that you need the card and the software, which is not cheap. You also need a lot of hard disk space – digitized video will take up a lot of space so it is a good idea to use computers that can copy clips to CD-ROM or ideally to DVD. Finally, you need to be aware of the copyright situation when using this kind of technology. In simple terms, recording a digital copy is no different from recording a copy of a programme on to VHS tape. The same restrictions also apply in terms of broadcasting and use. If you are showing clips to students and not charging or otherwise claiming that you hold the rights to the material then you are unlikely to infringe any copyright on the material. An increasing number of companies now supply this equipment. Two well established companies are Hauppage (http://www.hauppage.com/) and Pinnacle Systems (http://www.pinnaclesys.com/).

WEBSITE
WEBSITE

British Pathe

WEBSITE

A far easier way to access large collections of digital video material is via the British Pathe website (http://www.britishpathe.com/). This site contains a catalogue of thousands of news clips, starting in the 1890s and ending in the 1970s. It is easy to search (the searching functions are examined in chapter 4 on pages 72–73). British Pathe is a commercial website designed to help researchers preparing television programmes. As a result, the clips are downloadable but there is a fee to use them. However, the clips are downloadable free of charge in a low resolution format which has a large British Pathe watermark on the clips. However, schools in England and Wales are able to access high quality clips without the watermark free of charge. This is one of the most exciting resources to become available to history teachers in many years. Finding an interesting source to start a lesson, whether it is unemployment in the 1930s, wartime evacuation or the impact of the Beatles in the 1960s is now child's play.

Hulton Archive

WEBSITE

http://www.hultonarchive.com (now hosted on the archival section of http://editorial.gettyimages.com)
The Hulton Archive is a large collection of still images but also holds a large collection of downloadable moving images, with similar restrictions to British Pathe. As it is an American archive it is especially useful to schools examining twentieth-century American history.

WEBSITE

German Archive Videos

http://www.dhm.de/lemo/suche/videos.html

This site is similar in structure and aim to the British Pathe website. It's all in German but many titles are obvious, so persevere; it's a marvellous collection of archive material. Downloads are only available at preview quality, so can be a bit fuzzy.

WEBSITE

The National Archives Learning Curve

Home page: http://www.learningcurve.gov.uk

Exhibitions: http://www.learningcurve.gov.uk/exhibitions.htm

Onfilm: http://www.learningcurve.gov.uk/onfilm/archive.htm

Many Learning Curve exhibitions contain moving image clips as sources. The Home Front 1939–45 contains a wide range of newsreel clips, information films and assorted morale boosting productions on a wide range of aspects of the Second World War. The new exhibition on the Cold War contains audio and video clips relating to many different aspects of the Cold War. They are primarily news based clips but they range from interviews with refugees from East Berlin to a North Korean film giving a perspective on the Korean War. In addition to the exhibitions, there is also a special section of the site devoted to moving image sources called Onfilm. Onfilm is divided into two main sections, a film archive and an activities section. The film archive pulls together a range of clips from different sources and organizes them under standard curriculum headings.

Fig 7.1   **Film archive menu on The National Archives' Onfilm resource**

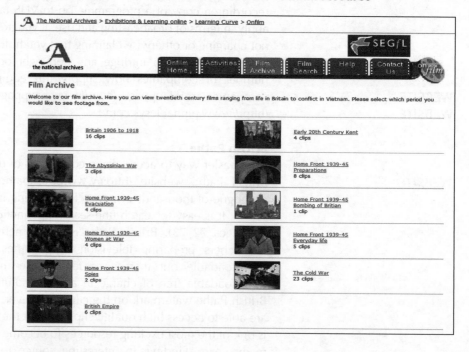

Screen Online

WEBSITE

Screen Online (http://www.screenonline.org.uk) is a resource managed by the British Film Institute, which provides a moving image history of British film and television. The emphasis is on the history of the medium from a media studies and English perspective. However, the material is organized by decade and as such provides a fascinating glimpse into what was informing and entertaining in each decade. The catalogue of clips can be viewed online, but the actual clips themselves can only be viewed from a school, library or similar institution. However, registration is free for such institutions.

WEBSITE

Moving History

Moving History (http://www.movinghistory.ac.uk) is similar to Screen Online in structure and intent, but it contains an interesting range of material drawn from local film archives across the country. These are helpfully divided into useful themes such as transport, conflict, art and culture.

BBC History

As you might expect, the BBC has a collection of video clips relating to history. They are mostly from the Simon Schama *History of Britain* series. There's no doubt they are well chosen, and the transformation of a modern church to its pre-Reformation glory is worth waiting the time it takes to load up. It's also one of the few places where digital video material relating to history is not solely confined to the twentieth century. If you are looking specifically for video materials, then your best approach is to go through the History Multimedia Zone, see figure 7.2 (http://www.bbc.co.uk/history/multimedia_zone/index.shtml). This index page will take you to the video collections and also the various animations, games, audio collections and other multimedia goodies on offer.

WEBSITE

Fig 7.2   **The front page of the BBC History Multimedia Zone**

BBC News

One area which might not immediately spring to mind but is also a source of interesting footage is the BBC News website (http://news.bbc.co.uk/). The majority of reports are clear and well written; they have useful links and also contain digital versions of reports used on the television news broadcasts. Most BBC reports use Real Player to play the clips. It can be downloaded free from http://uk.real.com/. There are some fairly obvious uses for these reports, particularly for schools tackling SHP courses or similar coursework studies which take historical issues right up to the present day. A less obvious, but equally valuable, aspect of the BBC News site is the archive of news coverage of anniversaries of historic events, such as the sixtieth anniversary of D-Day in 2004. The search facility for the news archive is pretty good at locating key words and giving you an idea what the articles found contain.

WEBSITE

WEBSITE

Commercial resources

With so many free sources of digital video available it may seem wasteful to consider spending money on commercial resources. The publishers of such resources are aware of this, and have created products which add value to the collections of clips they hold. One way in which they do this is that the quality of clip available on CD-ROM as opposed to an online connection is much higher. Another is the provision of an educational pathway through the material and ideas for the use of the material.

➡ Channel 4 CLIPBANK

WEBSITE

http://www.channel4.com/learning/index.html
Currently only on CD-ROM but with plans to be an online service as well.

➡ Nelson Thornes History Live

WEBSITE

http://www.nelsonthornes.com/secondary/history/books_history_live.htm
History Live is a commercial resource published by Nelson Thornes. It consists of a large collection of clips from the ITN archive on CD-ROM. It is organized into 12 assignments and accessed by a content management system.

Although useful, having access to collections of video clips will not teach any student or encourage students to think critically about moving images as a source. As with any other resource, digital video needs to be used in a planned and structured way.

Activities using digital video

Digital video is an excellent resource for starting off a lesson. It can also be useful in illustrating events and even attitudes in a way that reading or talking cannot. Obscure clips can be useful for puzzling and intriguing students and getting them wondering what the explanation is for the activity being shown. With careful questioning a teacher can use a small batch of digital video clips and a data projector to good effect. Some possible questions are:

➡ How realistic was the reportage?

➡ What was the aim of the reportage?

➡ What insight do films give us into contemporary values and thoughts?

➡ How are/were films made?

➡ What did the audience want/enjoy?

➡ Is there more to archive film than moving wallpaper?

➡ Compare the film with your own knowledge of the historical period shown.

➡ How has the film added to your understanding of the period?

➡ Do you think there is anything important that has been left out?

➡ How does the film represent the main historical characters and groups?

➡ Why do you think they were represented in the way they were?

➡ Make a list of the advantages and disadvantages of the film as a resource for historians.

➡ What do you think was the film maker's point of view?

Apart from questioning, there are many different activities involving digital video which might be termed theoretical, practical or potentially either one. In this instance – practical implies that the students will be using editing software or some other software tool to create a product involving digital video – theoretical implies that the students will carry out the same thinking and discussion which the practical task might involve but for whatever reasons it is not possible to create a video product.

Activity	Theoretical	Practical
Make a news report from the time	✓	✓
Make a guide to using film sources	✓	✓
Documentary from present day perspective (about the events, about the film)	✓	✓
Demonstrate that film/history is a construct – take liberties		✓
Transposing styles of film making/reportage		✓
Create a storyboard from clips (reverse storyboarding)	✓	
Analyse relationship between film and other sources in other media	✓	✓
Would clip X be made today?	✓	
Storyboard your own film	✓	
Analyse a clip as you would any other kind of source	✓	✓
Video diaries	✓	✓
Add music, soundtracks and so on		✓
Create film about specific events/locations	✓	✓
Advise a company on the best clips to use for a film on …	✓	✓
Sell an idea for a film to …	✓	✓
Being a researcher	✓	
Turn a talking head or other interpretation into a presentation	✓	✓

▌Hollywood and history

One of the most engaging ways to make use of digital video is to get students to examine Hollywood films as historical interpretations. This is probably the closest thing that a teacher can get to a lesson which is guaranteed to engage students. In addition, it is often possible to get hold of trailers and clips from websites promoting the films or from the sites of movie enthusiasts such as Reel Classics (http://www.reelclassics.com/). It is important that using Hollywood film does not degenerate into a rather futile exercise in spotting minor continuity errors such as a Roman emperor wearing a wristwatch. These are undoubtedly entertaining, and indeed spotting a few such errors can be an excellent way of showing students what you are not looking for! An excellent source of such errors can be found at The Nitpickers Site (http://www.nitpickers.com/) because of the range of errors listed in the films and also because it is fully aware of how trivial the nit-picking exercise is.

WEBSITE

WEBSITE

For most teachers, the main aim of using Hollywood film is to examine the interpretation of historical events or characters. It is here that digital video really starts to come into its own. Unlike VHS, movies on DVD can be bookmarked. Since you are unlikely to want or be able to show a complete movie to a class, the ability to mark key scenes in a film and find them easily is extremely useful. Alternatively, you may use the PVR or PC television technology described on page 137 in this chapter to digitize the actual clips you want to show and put these on a CD-ROM to be played and referred to. An extra dimension added by use of the computer is the fact that the internet is the home to a worldwide community of movie buffs and historians. This means that virtually any film ever made has usually accumulated a body of reviews.

Oliver Cromwell and the British Civil Wars

In this example, the existence of reviews turned out to be extremely useful. I was able to use digital recordings of selected extracts of two films. One was the movie *Cromwell* starring Richard Harris and made in 1970. The other was *To Kill a King* made in 2003. The extracts from these films were carefully selected to help students analyse a selection of reviews of the films. To begin with, the whole class looked at the first review, which was very short and uncontroversial.

Review 1: Review of *Cromwell* from the movie site Movies2Go.Net

WEBSITE　　http://www.movies2go.net/review/Cromwell.html

File Edit View Go Favorites Tools Window Help　　　　　　　　　Internet Explorer

Movies2Go　　　　　　　　　　　　　　　　　　　　　　Search

Setting: Great Britain in the 17th Century
Main Characters: Oliver Cromwell, King Charles I, Earl of
　　Manchester, Queen Henrietta Maria, John Carter, Prince Rupert,
　　Earl of Strafford, and Hugh Peters
Contains nothing offensive
Produced by Irwin Allen; Columbia Pictures
Screenplay by Ken Hughes and Ronald Haswood
Music: Frank Cordell
Special Effects: Bill Warrington
Special Categories: Academy Awards®; British Movies; Duels; True
　　Stories; Rulers; Kings and Queens;
Academy Awards®:
　　Costume Design - Nino Novarese
Academy Award® **Nominations:**
　　Original Musical Score (Dramatic) - Frank Cordell

　　The historical battle between Oliver Cromwell, the revolutionary and King Charles I has great cinematography but falls short on story.

Students then worked in groups and were given a review to read and reflect on, and decide whether or not the review was a fair reflection based on the clips seen. Not surprisingly, few students quibbled with the first review because there was so little to quibble with. Then the fun started, using some fairly brutal reviews, extracts of which are shown below.

Review 2: Review of *Cromwell* by Professor Blair Worden published on the Channel 4 History Heads site. The rating scale was 0–10 with 0 being truly terrible

WEBSITE   http://www.channel4.com/history/microsites/H/history/heads/pastimperfect/pastcromwell.html

File Edit View Go Favorites Tools Window Help   *Internet Explorer*

| NEWS | FILM | HOMES | LIFE | ENTERTAINMENT | HISTORY | SCIENCE | COMMUNITY | SHOP |
| SPORT | CULTURE | CARS | MONEY | BROADBAND | LEARNING | HEALTH | DATING | GAMES |

PAST IMPERFECT

Cromwell

Reviewed by Blair Worden, professor of history at the School of English and American Studies at the University of Sussex and author of Roundhead Reputations: The English Civil Wars and the passions of posterity *(Allen Lane, 2001)*

RATING: 4

British, 1970
Screenwriter/director Ken Hughes
Cinematographer Geoffrey Unsworth
Music Frank Cordell
Cast Richard Harris (Cromwell), Alec Guinness (Charles I), Robert Morley (Earl of Manchester), Dorothy Tutin, Frank Finlay, Timothy Dalton, Patrick Wymark, Patrick Magee, Nigel Stock, Charles Gray, Michael Jayston, Anna Cropper, Michael Goodliffe

How much obligation lies on makers of historical films to keep to the historical record? How much fiction is permissible within the representation of fact? No cinematic description of the past, and certainly not one designed for a mass audience, could be expected to stay within the boundary of the known. The pace of fiction cannot be the pace of life. Complexities of chronology will need reduction. Buildings and landscapes that contained historical events have disappeared. Dialogue must be invented. Characterisation may need to be simplified.

But elaboration and modification are one thing: perversion of fact is another. Claims for artistic licence could not warrant the wilful and almost unrelenting misrepresentations of *Cromwell*, which, whatever else it is, is not art, and which invites us to suppose, through a voice-over, that its account is historically authentic.

Cromwell in *Cromwell*

We begin in 1640, in Cambridge, where Cromwell (of Huntingdonshire and Ely) is supposed to live – perhaps because American viewers will have heard of it. The Irish rebellion of 1641 has already taken place; the Scottish war of 1639 has yet to start. Cromwell, instead of having grown poorer in recent years, has become a prosperous squire.

Reviews 3–4: These were reviews of *To Kill a King* posted on the Amazon website which was selling the film on DVD

WEBSITE   http://www.amazon.co.uk – then look up 'To Kill a King'

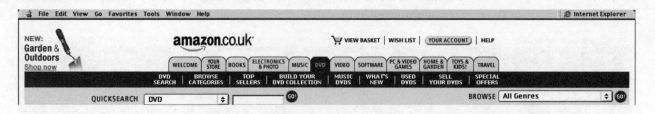

Customer Reviews

Avg. Customer Review: ★★☆☆☆

<u>Write an online review</u> and share your thoughts with other shoppers!

I can only echo the disappointment of previous reviewers. 'To Kill a King' is easy on the eye but historically grossly inaccurate. Anyone familiar with the actual events of the English Civil War period will soon be left seething at the 'poetic licence' taken by this production. The story appears to be set in an alternative universe version of the English Civil War where people's names, ages, and physical presence at specific historical events are randomly reallocated to present a vaguely familiar but very whimsical version of history. It concerns me that some may take the film at face value and believe it to be an accurate representation of historical events. It is not! I was left feeling sad and disappointed that a potentially excellent period piece was ruined for me by the lack of respect for history itself.

I had great hopes for this movie, but am very pleased I only viewed it on video rather than paying to see it at the cinema.

The acting is OK, the costumes are fine and the battle scenes enjoyable but the screen play is terrible.

Historically a travesty of the truth. It makes Cromwell out as some groupie hanging on to every word and deed of Fairfax. The film eventually goes so far as to dress up Cromwell as some black leather coated Nazi, looks like the writer was trying to draw some parallel with Hitler and modern history.

If you are looking for a historical costume drama with a passing nod to the true facts then watch it, otherwise I would look elsewhere, the 1970 movie Cromwell starring Richard Harris for example

Most teachers will see the fascinating possibilities that these reviews offer in terms of analysing the movies as historical interpretations, particularly the two reviews of *To Kill a King.* In this exercise, students were asked to study the reviews and suggest which scenes from the clips shown might be selected by the reviewers to support their case. This discussion was then followed by concentrating on Worden's opening point in review 2 about the intentions and responsibilities of the film maker. In order to support this discussion, students were presented with a final review commenting on the wider issues of film literacy. An extract is shown opposite. It is very challenging stuff intellectually, but it does raise the critical issue of how we often invoke the past, or section of the past which suits us, in order to explain or justify a present day situation.

Review 5: Extract from a review of *Cromwell* on the website Popmatters.com

WEBSITE

http://www.popmatters.com/film/reviews/c/cromwell.shtml

> But although this interpretation of Cromwell is wholly invented, the number of history teachers posting enthusiastic reviews of this movie on sites like amazon.com and Internet Movie Database (imdb.com) suggests that Hughes' fantasy of Cromwell is alive, well, and ideologically active (maybe even in the classroom). Add that to the popular disillusion with the cost of the-war-after-the-war in Iraq and the propensity to blame a hectoring administration which was dishonest about its motives for invasion for the debacle, and the urge to look beyond the traditional political classes for 21st century leadership may prove compelling. In a nation where a World War II general served two Presidential terms less than fifty years ago, where messianic media speculation attended the potential U.S. Presidential candidacy of General Colin Powell, and the real candidacy of "war hero" John McCain, and has now resurged to envelop Wesley Clark, the reinforcement of the image of the citizen-soldier-democrat as a purer and more altruistic politician (even when it shows up in a 30-year-old movie like *Cromwell*) is a powerful political act.
>
> The susceptibility of contemporary America to this image undoubtedly comes from its persistent rewriting of its own revolution (in which an aristocratic oligarchy successfully paid lip service to the rights of all in return for the concentration of national power in the hands of the few, and managed to spin George Washington's return to his slave-run plantation into a resumption of life as a simple farmer) as a triumph for the "ordinary" American. In light of this, and given the current situation in Iraq, Hughes' willful remaking of the civil wars and revolutions in 17th-century Britain is a far more potent obfuscator of rational political debate today than it was in 1970.

How did the Poor Law get its dark reputation?

This last theme was also explored in this investigation into the historical reputation of the Poor Law following the Amendment Act in 1834. Reputation is an excellent vehicle for making the study of historical interpretations accessible to students. Almost all students will understand that people they know, or perhaps film stars, may have reputations which may or may not be deserved. The Poor Law certainly has a grim reputation because of its associations with the misery of the workhouse. This image engages powerfully with the emotional side of learning and makes a lasting impact on students' memory. However, in this instance, the emotional basis for this reputation is somewhat at odds with what academic historians are saying about it. This became the basis for the learning package set out in figure 7.3. The emphasis was not just on the reality of the workhouse but also the way in which authors of material such as film actually play on the emotions in order to create a memorable impression.

Fig 7.3   Learning package on the historical reputation of the Poor Law

CD–ROM Ch 7/Poor Law – Fraser
extract Word doc

How did the Poor Law get its dark reputation?

Stage 1: A simple survey

This involved students asking family, friends, other students:

- whether they had ever heard of the Poor Law, workhouses and so on
- what they thought of the Poor Law if they had heard of it
- if they could say where they got their information from.

Stage 2: Study of the views of a modern historian

Here students studied the following amended extract from *The Evolution of the British Welfare State* by Professor Derek Fraser.

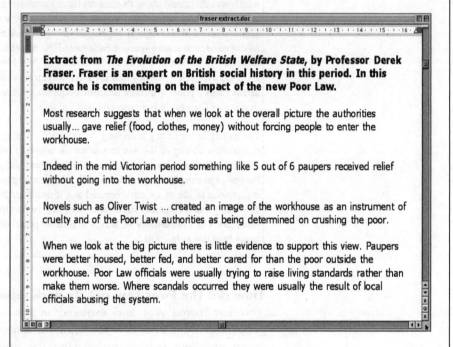

Extract from *The Evolution of the British Welfare State*, by Professor Derek Fraser. Fraser is an expert on British social history in this period. In this source he is commenting on the impact of the new Poor Law.

Most research suggests that when we look at the overall picture the authorities usually... gave relief (food, clothes, money) without forcing people to enter the workhouse.

Indeed in the mid Victorian period something like 5 out of 6 paupers received relief without going into the workhouse.

Novels such as Oliver Twist ... created an image of the workhouse as an instrument of cruelty and of the Poor Law authorities as being determined on crushing the poor.

When we look at the big picture there is little evidence to support this view. Paupers were better housed, better fed, and better cared for than the poor outside the workhouse. Poor Law officials were usually trying to raise living standards rather than make them worse. Where scandals occurred they were usually the result of local officials abusing the system.

Students were asked to ponder how this view differed from the popular view of the Poor Law and why this difference might exist.

Stage 3: Study a clip from the 1948 movie *Oliver Twist*

Students had already used extracts from the Dickens novel as primary source material. In stage 1, they generally found that people had heard of the novel but generally because it had been turned into a movie! After watching the clip, students were asked to identify the ways in which the director had created a particular impression of the Poor Law officials and the workhouse. In this exercise, a handy feature of digital video was the ability to pause a clip and get a clean view of the frame without the usual buzzing or jumping in the picture when a VHS recording is paused. Frames can usually be copied as well to create still images.

Stage 4: Study a clip from the 1968 musical movie *Oliver Twist*

With this clip students were asked to consider the ways in which the earlier film had influenced the later film. A detailed analysis made this strikingly clear. The Poor Law officials were re-created in very similar ways. This pointed to the ways in which the earlier film had laid down a popular understanding of the workhouse which was then reinforced by the 1968 film.

Stage 5: A visual from the original edition of *Oliver Twist*

This final twist was designed to get students to see how careful we must be to avoid taking movies as factual record. In both the 1948 and 1968 movies, Oliver Twist is invariably dressed in rags and is barefoot. In the illustration below from the British Library CD-ROM *Britain 1750–1900*, the illustration from the book *Oliver Twist* shows Oliver reasonably well dressed and wearing shoes.

Getting a sense of period

Life in the trenches

News footage can be just as effective as Hollywood movies in whole-class teaching. Figure 7.4 shows some slides from a PowerPoint presentation created by a teacher in Northern Ireland working on a project run by the Northern Ireland Film and Television Commission (http://www.niftc.co.uk/). In this lesson, the students were being asked to consider the impact of war on the new recruits from different parts of Ireland. The underlined words in the presentation are hyperlinks to archive clips showing different experiences of various Irish regiments in the war. In this instance, the teacher was carefully guiding the students in the use of moving image sources by carefully planning the task and just as carefully selecting the clips to be used.

WEBSITE

Fig 7.4   **Four slides from the presentation 'Life in the trenches'**

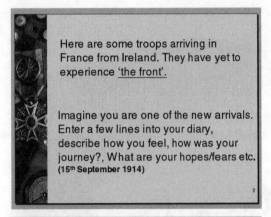

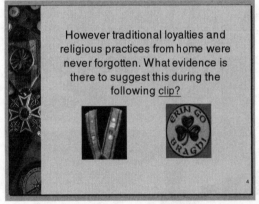

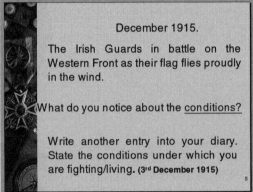

Soundtracks and genres

Studying the soundtracks of video clips is one of the easiest and most effective ways to get students to start thinking of moving image sources as sources rather than as information which is value free and to be accepted unquestioningly. For many students this is quite a conceptual leap. Much of the video that students see (from television history programmes) is simply used as background 'moving wallpaper' to accompany a soundtrack read by a narrator. The essence of the footage itself as a source is almost never analysed or even referred to. This is a great pity since it loses out on the potential value of much moving image as historical source. It also misses an opportunity to use this medium to engage the students in activities which lend themselves beautifully to the VAK approach.

The Model T Ford

In this instance, I used a clip from an internet resource that was a one minute advertisement from 1923 for the Model T Ford. The aim was to explore the soundtrack and it turned out to be a fruitful line of enquiry.

➡ After studying the USA economy in the 1920s we then focused in on the motor industry. At the first pass, this clip provided a neat activity by simply turning off the sound and asking the students to write a one minute soundtrack. That was a fun activity and they all wrote sensible soundtracks in a documentary genre.

➡ Interestingly, not one student wrote in the advertisement genre. So, when I then played the clip with the soundtrack we discussed the differences between their use of the clip and the actual use.

➡ We also looked at how both the genres of soundtrack went well with the clip. This is where the ability to advance digital clips one frame at a time really comes into its own. The students were able to see how the different styles of soundtrack correlated differently (but effectively) to different events in the clip.

➡ There was yet more mileage to be gained from this clip. As a finishing off exercise students were asked to create another soundtrack. This time they had to write a script for a film that was trying to explain that in many ways the story of the motor industry in 1920s' USA was representative of the booming USA economy as a whole.

More soundtrack tasks

Two activities and a discussion from a one minute clip seemed like pretty good value! In fact, this is just the start of the mileage that can be gained from activities based around soundtracks. Another really interesting activity is to get students to work on the same clip and experiment with the impact of different voice-overs on the clip. I have tried this out with silent clips from the Great War in which students write and read out voice-overs which present the traditional 'Blackadder' view of the Great War and then read out voice-overs which stress the positive aspects of wartime experience that contemporary sources often refer to. It would be easy enough to replicate this task to other circumstances. Students might write and read out contrasting voice-overs on clips showing evacuation in the Second World War, the impact of bombing and the importance of the creation of the National Health Service. Of course, writing and reading out soundtracks is a rather low tech approach to this activity. In an ideal situation, students would be recording their voice-overs, editing them on to the soundtrack using video editing software and then playing them back to the class. Whether the high or low tech approach is used, the key learning experience is the discussion. It is very challenging but also quite thought provoking to get students explaining how a completely different story can be told using exactly the same video clip. This technique can be very powerful in getting students to realize that most programmes and films are constructed to say what the film maker wants, rather than necessarily being faithful to reports of what actually happened.

News footage as primary sources

A recurring theme in this chapter is the use of moving images as primary source materials. This can be a powerful way of involving students in source work, which research suggests is one of their least favourite activities. For many students, one reason for this dislike is that source work generally involves analysing written texts. However, selected news clips can be very powerful in getting students to see the subtext of video clips and getting them to see that video and text sources can complement each other very powerfully. It is here that the VHS and even the projector become less useful than students accessing their own collections of clips, either on their own or in small group-work.

The Cuban Crisis

A good example of a video text is President Kennedy's speech of October 1962 in which he announced the existence of Soviet missiles on Cuba and set out what he planned to do about it. Figure 7.5 shows a screen from the History Live collection of clips relating to the Cuban Crisis, containing the source in question.

Fig 7.5   **Screen from the Nelson Thornes *History Live* assignment on the Cuban Crisis. Students click on the thumbnail to play the video clip**

Using software such as this, or perhaps a similar source from British Pathe or other free resources, students could be set the task of analysing Kennedy's speech in much the same way as they would be asked to analyse a transcript of it. Again, we see the potential of moving image to engage students in what is essentially a text based task in a medium (sound and moving image) with which they are naturally more comfortable. The speech is ideal for asking students to explain how Kennedy tries to justify the legitimacy of his actions to his audience. The difference in this instance is that students can play and replay the clip as often as they need to gain the understanding they are looking for – clearly not possible if the only way to view the clip is on a projector or a VHS player.

Vietnam War

In examinations, students are often asked to consider two or more sources and explain which is more valuable or useful to the historian examining a particular topic. Bringing in digital video can make this type of exercise a powerful multimedia experience. Students asked to examine a scene from a movie based on the Vietnam War (such as *Apocalypse Now*) might struggle to explain how valuable this is as a source for the historian. However, faced with additional sources which support or contradict the impression given in the movie clip and the exercise becomes a familiar one, but with the added advantage of making use of what is for many students a more attractive medium. Thus the famous speech from *Apocalypse Now* in which Marlon Brando claims that the USA simply cannot beat the Vietcong because they never give up, might be tested against contemporary written sources but also extracts from contemporary news footage. Both this exercise and the one on Cuba could be taken to another level again if students were able to use video editing software to extract the key sections of clips in just the same way that they would highlight key sections of text on a word processor. Here again our kinesthetic learner would probably be in his/her element in using the full sensory range and using some fancy software to create the end product. One of the most easy to use and flexible tools for this type of activity is QuickTime Pro. This is an upgraded version of the QuickTime player that is free and commonly available on most computers. Figure 7.6 provides a small glimpse of what QuickTime Pro can do. More details about this software are available from the QuickTime website

WEBSITE (http://www.apple.com/quicktime/).

Fig 7.6   **Some features of QuickTime Pro**

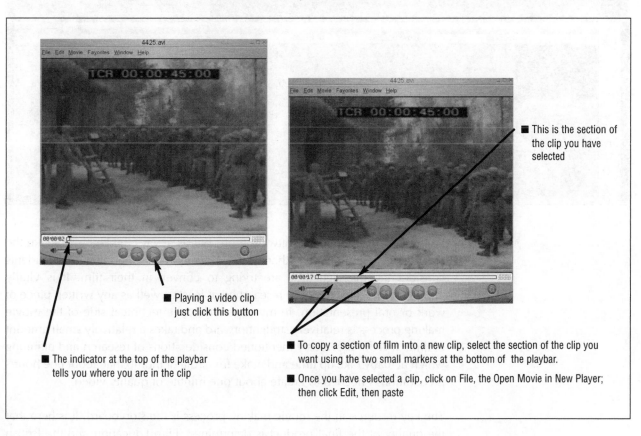

■ The indicator at the top of the playbar tells you where you are in the clip

■ Playing a video clip just click this button

■ This is the section of the clip you have selected

■ To copy a section of film into a new clip, select the section of the clip you want using the two small markers at the bottom of the playbar.

■ Once you have selected a clip, click on File, the Open Movie in New Player; then click Edit, then paste

Making movies

QuickTime Pro is just one of several excellent software tools available for the most exciting possibility which digital video offers – making your own documentaries. Another widely used package is Studio 9 from Pinnacle Systems, as seen in figure 7.7 (http://www.pinnaclesys.com). Other products are mad by companies such as Roxio (http://www.roxio.com/). Then there is the iMovie software (http://www.apple.com/ilife/imovie/) for Macintosh machines and it is also worth remembering that Windows Moviemaker comes free of charge with the Windows XP operating system from Microsoft.

WEBSITE
WEBSITE
WEBSITE

Fig 7.7   **Editing suite for Pinnacle Studio 9. Clips are dragged from the album area into the time line and then edited. Voice and music soundtracks can be added. So can text commentaries that run along the top or bottom of the clip. There are many other effects which can be added. Most applications use a layout similar to this one**

So there is no shortage of software tools, but as always the key is to make the creation of the film more than just a novelty. It is important that students consider the message they are trying to convey in their film. It is vitally important that their films are researched at least as well as any written piece of work or oral presentation. In my experience, the technical side of the movie making process is relatively straightforward and takes a relatively small amount of time. It is the previously mentioned considerations of research and planning which actually take up time and make for a rule of thumb that about one hour's preparation is needed to create about one minute of quality video.

The key resource in the movie making process is the storyboard. It is here that the quality of the final product is determined. Film Education and the British Film Institute both supply free resources which provide ideas and templates about the process of storyboarding. However, storyboarding does not need to be hugely sophisticated. Figure 7.8 shows the scripts published online by the production company which made the Channel 4 series on the Great War. It separates out the visual elements from the narrative and commentary elements of the script.

Fig 7.8   **Extract from the scripts for the Channel 4 series on the Great War**

The First World War Prog 6 - 50' Final Script - Website	1
Episode 6 – Breaking the Deadlock	
Pre title sequence	
Archive B/w film footage/guns fire/men struggle through mud/trench scenes	**Comm 1** **10 00 22** *Think of the First World War, and you think of trenches.* **10 00 28** *There was mobility elsewhere: in the East and Africa. But the war on the Western Front was bogged down.* **10 00 37** *The challenge on both sides was to find new ideas, new weapons, new spirit among the men. Only then could they break out - and win.*
Series title, opening sequence & episode title	
Caption 1 THE FIRST WORLD WAR	**10 00 51**
Caption 2 Episode Six BREAKING THE DEADLOCK	**10 01 21**

Figure 7.9 shows a learning package about the Victorians which uses a similar approach but with slight amendments. This exercise took place at the Park View City Learning Centre in Birmingham. In the first stage of the exercise, students examined the downside of Victorian Britain and, in character, explained the worst aspects. This gained added spice as they were filmed against a green screen which allowed the technology to drop in a Victorian background after the students delivered their talks. Not surprisingly, when this task was completed the kinesthetic learners rather stole the show, but the whole exercise offered something to the students with different learning styles. The teachers of several classes commented on the fact that the material was strongly visual. The storyboard came in the second stage where students then looked at the not so bad side of life. They presented their understanding of this either by planning and creating their own film or (under teacher guidance) they used the ready prepared script. They selected sections from this script and then located still and moving image clips to go with it, recorded the soundtrack and put the whole package together.

Fig 7.9 Extracts from tasks on the Victorians used to examine the good and bad side of Victorian Britain. Part of the package is available on the CD-ROM which accompanies the book; however, for copyright reasons are unable to include the film clips used in the original exercise

CD-ROM Ch 7/Victorian times bad Word doc

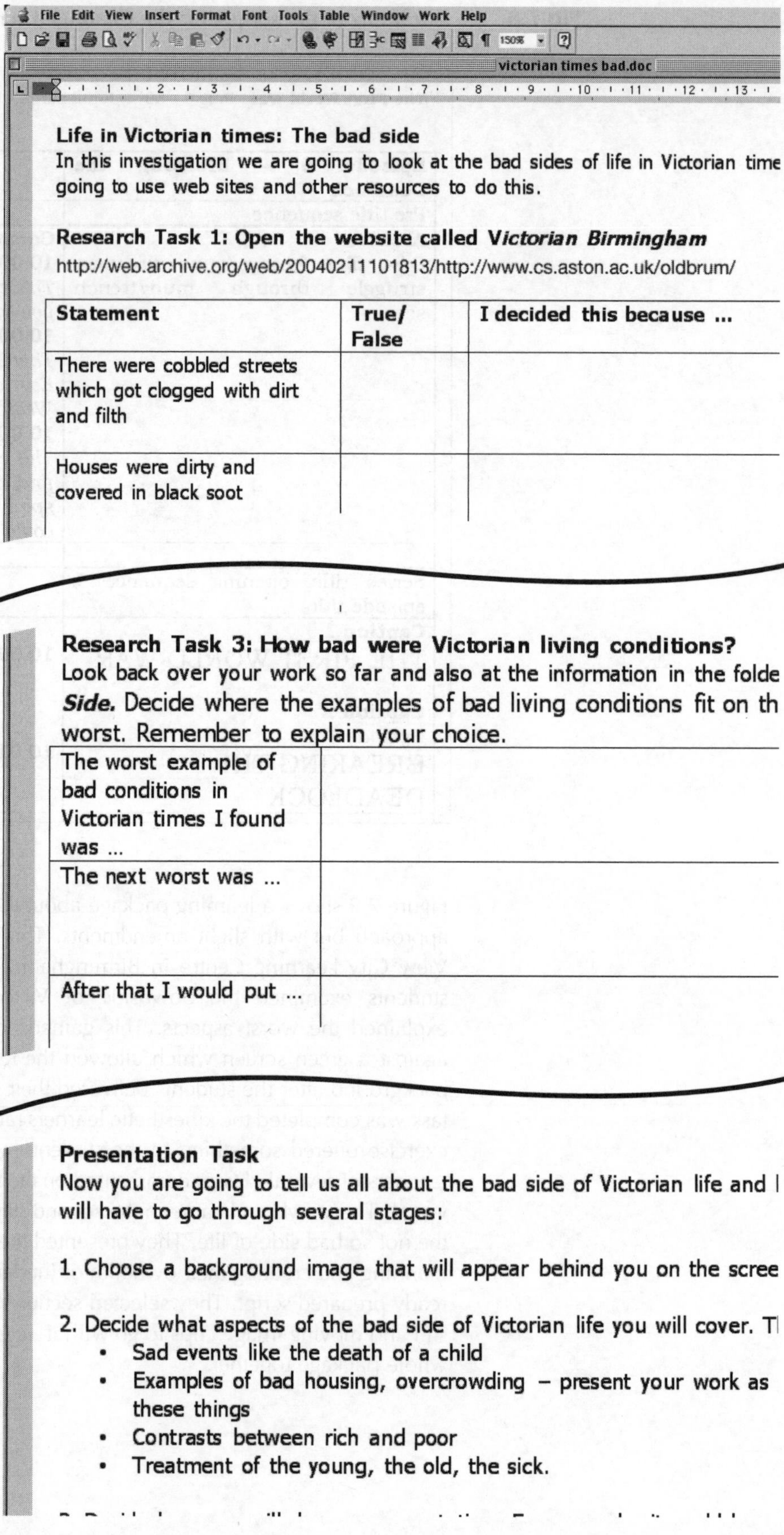

File Edit View Insert Format Font Tools Table Window Work Help

victorian times bad.doc

Life in Victorian times: The bad side
In this investigation we are going to look at the bad sides of life in Victorian time going to use web sites and other resources to do this.

Research Task 1: Open the website called *Victorian Birmingham*
http://web.archive.org/web/20040211101813/http://www.cs.aston.ac.uk/oldbrum/

Statement	True/ False	I decided this because ...
There were cobbled streets which got clogged with dirt and filth		
Houses were dirty and covered in black soot		

Research Task 3: How bad were Victorian living conditions?
Look back over your work so far and also at the information in the folde *Side.* Decide where the examples of bad living conditions fit on th worst. Remember to explain your choice.

The worst example of bad conditions in Victorian times I found was ...	
The next worst was ...	
After that I would put ...	

Presentation Task
Now you are going to tell us all about the bad side of Victorian life and I will have to go through several stages:

1. Choose a background image that will appear behind you on the scree

2. Decide what aspects of the bad side of Victorian life you will cover. T
   • Sad events like the death of a child
   • Examples of bad housing, overcrowding – present your work as these things
   • Contrasts between rich and poor
   • Treatment of the young, the old, the sick.

Figure 7.10 shows a similar exercise aimed at older students. Here they have to create a news broadcast in what is effectively a newsroom simulation. It is not hard to see how such a task would motivate the vast majority of students, but again it's worth noting the importance of the storyboard in making sure that the end product is good quality history and that there is some kind of angle over and above a narrative of the war. It is a high technology exercise which will interest teachers looking to develop ICT skills both in the use of software but also in the way that software and presentation impact on an audience. These are goals of teaching and learning in ICT as well as in history, which seems a fitting point to end the chapter.

Fig 7.10   A newsroom simulation activity on the Vietnam War

Why were the USA and its allies not able to defeat the Vietcong in the Vietnam War?

Briefing

It is April 1975. Communist forces from North Vietnam have just taken over Saigon, the capital of South Vietnam. The last American troops and officials were lifted out by helicopter in an embarrassing scramble as the North Vietnamese troops approached. The main American forces left Vietnam two years ago, partly because of the heavy losses they were suffering.

Stage 1: Your assignment

Your assignment is to prepare a five minute television news report on the fall of Saigon.
Your main angle is:

● The USA and South Vietnam forces had more money, more troops, better equipment, better food and better medicines than the Vietcong. So how come they didn't win?

Stage 2: Your research

1. Look at all the available clips (using the play list), and browse the other folders to see what images and sounds are available. If you need more images you can get these from the websites listed in the Links page.

2. Plan your report using a storyboard. When you start using the storyboard don't use the link again. It will start a new blank storyboard. Keep updating your storyboard in Word.

3. Go to the editing studio and start selecting clips, recording voice-overs, editing selections and producing your report.

Stage 3: Your storyboard

Here are some of the issues and areas you could cover in your report. You may not be able to cover all this in a five minute report. You will have to decide which of these points will feature in greater depth and which will be skimmed over.

● Why it seemed the USA was certain to win

● USA tactics in Vietnam

● USA weaknesses

● Vietcong strengths

● Lack of support for USA involvement in war

● Conclusion: What you think were the most important factors and how these factors linked together.

Story board section	Clips which are relevant to this section and which could be used	What viewer will see	What viewer will hear	Notes
1	275	USA troops and officials fleeing Saigon 1975	These scenes show how American and South Vietnamese plans went so badly wrong. We see …	
		Now it's over to you!		
2				
3				
4				
5				

Chapter 8

Getting help and support

Concluding thoughts: Where to go from here?

It is hoped that somewhere in chapters 1–7 of this book there are some ideas, practical activities, resources or just aspirations which have inspired the reader to either start using ICT to enhance teaching and learning in history or to take current practice into new and interesting areas. Clearly a book like this cannot begin to anticipate all of the challenges and opportunities that will face each teacher in each school. Fortunately, there is a useful network of support which can provide advice, ideas and hopefully useful resources to help you meet these challenges.

Innovating History

WEBSITE

http://www.qca.org.uk/history/innovating/

This site has been developed by the history team at the Qualifications and Curriculum Authority as part of a three year development project for history for 4–19 year olds. Innovating History contains a wide range of information updates, exemplars for planning in history, case studies of successful practice and a huge range of other valuable material. It does not have a primary focus on the use of ICT, but ICT examples are part of the range of areas it covers.

Historical Association

WEBSITE

http://www.history.org.uk

Recent government policy has been to involve subject associations as much as possible in the development of teaching and learning in subjects, and particularly in the embedding of ICT in good teaching and learning practice. The Historical Association has developed a high level of expertise in this area, with a dedicated subject officer and a range of publications and training courses as part of what it can offer.

Schools History Project

WEBSITE

http://www.tasc.ac.uk/shp/

The SHP has long been a source of innovation in curriculum development and classroom practice. The SHP website contains a range of useful links and case studies, including the use of ICT, most of which are specific to the content of SHP examination courses. There is also information about the annual SHP conference, many of whose sessions are ICT based.

WEBSITE

DfES ICT in Schools

http://www.dfes.gov.uk/ictinschools/

The Department for Education and Skills has placed a high priority on the development of ICT in schools as a discrete subject and also as a resource to enhance work in school subjects. This site is an excellent way to keep abreast of developments in ICT generally. It is also a good place to find links to other organizations and materials which may be of use.

WEBSITE

BECTA

http://www.becta.org.uk/

WEBSITE

The role of the British Educational Communications and Technology Agency is to promote the use of ICT in the classroom. This large site is subdivided into subsections, each of which is aimed at specific audiences. Under the schools headings you will find resources such as the ICT advice site (http://www.ictadvice.org.uk/). This very handy resource contains discussion forums, articles, resources, case studies and a wealth of other materials to provide advice, encouragement and stimulation.

School History Forum

WEBSITE

http://www.schoolhistory.co.uk/forum/

This resource has been mentioned several times in the book already, but deserves a further mention. It is stimulating and informative, but also extremely supportive. It is not hard to find examples where a member of the forum has asked for help and been bombarded with advice and ideas. This is what internet communities are all about!

RBCs and LEAs

WEBSITE

RBCs are Regional Broadband Consortia (http://broadband.ngfl.gov.uk/). These are essentially co-operatives of LEAs (local education authorities). They are divided into regional grids whose role is to provide the hardware, software and educational support to help schools make the most effective use of fast broadband internet connections. From the RBC home page you can select your region and see what each regional grid has to offer. For most teachers interested in history, there are likely to be two areas of interest. One is the general ICT support, which can be offered by the specialist advisers in each LEA (these are also linked from the RBC home page). The second is the work of the content manager for each grid. This person is the key contact in terms of what resources are bought and/or developed by each regional grid. The big advantage of these grids is their size and buying power combined with their local focus. Thus, the North West Grid for Learning has supported a number of initiatives, including an oral history project that created video interviews of many people's experiences of living in and around Manchester during the 1940s and 1950s. The London Grid for Learning has made census data for all London boroughs in 1891 available – just one of a wide range of London history resources. The South West

WEBSITE

Grid for Learning has bought a subscription to the ProQuest Learning Service (http://www.proquest.co.uk) for all schools in the south west. ProQuest is a huge and extremely rich resource of historical content and teaching materials. It is scrupulous about collecting material and protecting the copyright of contributors and so is expensive – out of range for many individual schools or departments, but accessible through an arrangement such as this. RBCs are one of the most dynamic forces driving quality resources and work in classrooms, and all teachers will gain something from finding out more about them.

References

Alfano, R (2000), 'Databases, spreadsheets and historical enquiry at Key Stage 3', *Teaching History*, 101, history and ICT edition, November, pp 42–47

Atkin, D (2000), 'How do I improve my use of ICT? Put history first!', *Teaching History*, 99, Curriculum Planning edition, May, pp 42–49

British Film Institute (2000), *Moving Images in the Classroom: A Secondary Teachers' Guide to Using Film and Television*, p 4

Counsell, C (1998), *Defining Effectiveness in History using ICT: Approaches to Successful Practice*, BECTA/HA

HABET (1992), *Teaching History using IT*, Historical Association Advisory Body on Educational Technology

Haydn, Terry and Counsell, Christine, eds, (2003), *History, ICT and Learning in the Secondary School*, Routledge Falmer

Haydn, T and Walsh, B (2002), 'Lessons from the blunt edge: using the word processor to help learners' analytical and discursive thinking in history', *History Computer Review* (USA), Autumn

Lachs, V (2000), *Making Multimedia in the Classroom*, Routledge Falmer

Laffin, D (2000), 'A poodle with bite: using ICT to make AS Level more rigorous', *Teaching History*, 101, history and ICT edition, November, pp 8–16

Lewis, M J and Lloyd Jones, R (1996), *Using Computers in history: A Practical Guide*, Routledge

Martin, D (1998), 'The Hopi is different from the Pawnee: using a datafile to explore pattern and diversity', *Teaching History*, 93, history and ICT edition, November, pp 22–27

NIFTC/BFI Education Policy Working Group (2004), *A Wider Literacy: The Case for Moving Image Media Education in Northern Ireland*, NIFTC/BFI

Ofsted (2000), *Subject Reports 1999-2000: history*

Ofsted (2000), *Subject Reports 1999-2000: Information Technology*

Ofsted (2004), *Subject Reports 2002-2003: history in primary schools*

Ofsted (2004), *Subject Reports 2002-2003: Information and communication technology in primary schools*

Ofsted (2004) *Subject Reports 2002-2003: history in secondary schools*

Ofsted (2004) *Subject Reports 2002-2003: Information and communication technology in secondary schools*

Pitt, J (2000), 'Computing on a shoestring: extending pupils' historical vision with limited resources', *Teaching History*, 101, history and ICT edition, November, pp 25–29

Rayner, L (1999), 'Weighing a century with a web site: teaching Year 9 to be critical', *Teaching History*, 96, citizenship and identity edition, August, pp 13–22

Riley, M (2000), 'Into the key stage 3 History garden: choosing and planting your enquiry questions', *Teaching History*, 99, March

Scott, H and Smith, R (2004), 'Critical Skills in History', *Times Educational Supplement Teacher Magazine*, 11 June 2004

Smart, L (1996), *Using IT in Primary School History*, Cassell

Smart, L (1998), 'Maps, ICT and history: A revolution in learning', *Teaching History*, 93, history and ICT edition, November, pp 28–31

Smith, Alistair (1996), *Accelerated Learning in Practice*, Network Educational Press

Smith, A and Call, N (1999), *Accelerated Learning in the Primary School: The ALPS Approach*, Network Educational Press

Smith, A, Lovatt, D and Wise, D (2003), *Accelerated Learning: A User's Guide*, Network Educational Press

Sutton, P (2001), 'Preparing for history teaching in the digital age', *Teaching History*, 102, motivation and inspiration edition, February, pp 45–47

Turtle, J (2000), 'Serving up documents whole', *Teaching History*, 101, history and ICT edition, November, p 48

Walsh, B (1998), 'Why Gerry likes history now: the power of the word processor', *Teaching History*, 93, history and ICT edition, November, pp 6–15

Weatherley, C, Bonney B, Kerr, J and Morrison, J (2003), *Transforming Teaching and Learning*, Network Educational Press

Wyse, L and Lucas, C (1997), *Atlas of World History for Young People*, Geddes & Grosset

Acknowledgements

Pages 10, 46
Illustrations by Katherine Baxter

Page 14, 16
Home page reproduced with permission from Derek Allen, Snaith Primary School
(http://home.freeuk.com/elloughton13/index.htm)

Page 17
'Harry's Day' reproduced with permission from The Sainsbury Archive, Arthur Robins illustrator.

Page 18
Home page reproduced with permission from Andrew Field (http://www.schoolhistory.co.uk).

Pages 19-20, 74-75
Writing frame, Living standards in London 1891, reproduced with permission by Lindsey Rayner and Asyia Kazmi.

Pages 25-26, 82, 83
Extracts from Haydn, T and Counsell, C, eds, (2003), *History, ICT and Learning in the Secondary School*, Routledge, reproduced by permission of Taylor & Francis

Pages 35, 148
Screen shot from 'African Empires: A continent with no history?' and the animation 'Islamic conquests in Africa 632–750' reproduced with the permission of Nelson Thornes Ltd from *History Live* and *Empires and Citizens* by Ben Walsh.

Page 44
Extract from Wyse, L and Lucas, C (1997) *Atlas of World History for Young People*, reproduced by permission of Geddes & Grossett

Page 46
Photos reproduced by permission of the Imperial War Museum, negative numbers Q9268, Q2453 and Q2607.

Page 56
Screen shot of 'The Sudenland, 1938' from the CD-ROM *GCSE Modern World History, Electronic Edition*, Hodder Murray (yet to be published), reproduced by permission of Hodder Murray.

Pages 59, 95, 96, 99
Screen shots of Victorian homes, Henry VIII, Cold War and Tudor Hackney reproduced with permission from The National Archives Learning Curve (http://www.learningcurve.gov.uk).

Pages 61, 62
'Ownership of land in Dorset before the Norman Conquest in 1066' and data files from the 'Domesday Book for Dorset in 1087', BECTA copyright material, developed jointly by BECTA and the Historical Association.

Page 65

Huntingdon Jail data set – material from Junior Viewpoint reproduced by permission of Logotron Ltd.

Page 83

Dan Moorhouse, website evaluation sheet 'Civil Wars in the 1630s–1640s', reproduced with permission from Dan Moorhouse. For more information on the history teachers discussion forum log onto http://www.schoolhistory.co.uk/forum.

Page 85

Cartoon image (left), unknown source.

Poster image (right) reproduced by permission of Bildarchiv Preußischer Kulturbesitz, Berlin, Germany.

Pages 88, 121

Screen shots from the British Museum's Children's COMPASS Online resource reproduced with permission from The British Museum; image copyright The British Museum COMPASS 2000.

Page 92

The Sainsbury Archive, Letter 'Engagement of Female Staff', 7 September 1939, typed copy file reproduced with permission from The Sainsbury Archive.

Page 97

Screen shot of a map of the Albert Dock, from the Mersey Gateway 'Gateway to Learning' (http://www.mersey-gateway.org/education).

Page 102

Web page reproduced by kind permission of Michael Farry.

Page 110

Robert Catesby web page reproduced with permission (http://www.gunpowder-plot.org).

Page 111

Figure 6.2 reproduced by permission of the British Library, shelfmark Stowe 956. Folio No: 1v-2.

Page 122

Screen shot of 'Reconstruction of a scene in the trenches in the Great War' from the CD-ROM *Essential GCSE Modern World History*, Hodder Murray, reproduced by permission of Hodder Murray.

Page 128

Panorama of Romsey Abbey reproduced by permission of Astarte Digital, www.astartedigital.com

Page 138

Film archive web page reproduced with permission from The National Archives (http://www.learningcurve.pro.gov.uk/onfilm/archive.htm).

Page 147

Illustration from the book *Oliver Twist* reproduced by permission of the British Library, shelfmark c131d26, vol 1, p.28.

Index

Exciting ICT in History

Other publications from Network Educational Press

ACCELERATED LEARNING SERIES
Accelerated Learning: A User's Guide by Alistair Smith, Mark Lovatt and Derek Wise
Accelerated Learning in Practice by Alistair Smith
The ALPS Approach: accelerated learning in primary schools by Alistair Smith and Nicola Call
The ALPS Approach Resource Book by Alistair Smith and Nicola Call
MapWise by Oliver Caviglioli and Ian Harris
Creating an Accelerated Learning School by Mark Lovatt and Derek Wise
ALPS StoryMaker by Stephen Bowkett
Thinking for Learning by Mel Rockett and Simon Percival
Reaching out to all learners by Cheshire LEA
Leading Learning by Alistair Smith
Bright Sparks by Alistair Smith
Move It by Alistair Smith
Coaching Solutions by Will Thomas and Alistair Smith

EFFECTIVE LEARNING AND LEADERSHIP
Effective Heads of Department by Phil Jones & Nick Sparks
Effective Learning Activities by Chris Dickinson
Lessons are for Learning by Mike Hughes
Classroom Management by Philip Waterhouse and Chris Dickinson
Raising Boys' Achievement by Jon Pickering
Closing the Learning Gap by Mike Hughes
Strategies for Closing the Learning Gap by Mike Hughes and Andy Vass
Tweak to Transform by Mike Hughes
Leading the Learning School by Colin Weatherley
Transforming Teaching and Learning by Colin Weatherley, Bruce Bonney, John Kerr and Jo Morrison
Effective Teachers by Tony Swainston
Effective Teachers in Primary Schools by Tony Swainston
Effective Leadership in Schools by Tony Swainston

ABLE AND TALENTED CHILDREN COLLECTION
Effective Provision for Able and Talented Children by Barry Teare
Effective Resources for Able and Talented Children by Barry Teare
More Effective Resources for Able and Talented Children by Barry Teare
Challenging Resources for Able and Talented Children by Barry Teare
Enrichment Activities for Able and Talented Children by Barry Teare

OTHER TITLES
Help Your Child To Succeed by Bill Lucas and Alistair Smith
The Thinking Child by Nicola Call with Sally Featherstone
The Thinking Child Resource Book by Nicola Call with Sally Featherstone
But Why? Developing philosophical thinking in the classroom by Sara Stanley with Steve Bowkett
Becoming Emotionally Intelligent by Catherine Corrie
That's Science!; That's Maths!; That's English! by Tim Harding
Foundations of Literacy by Sue Palmer and Ros Bayley
With Drama in Mind by Patrice Baldwin
Imagine That... by Stephen Bowkett
Self-Intelligence by Stephen Bowkett
Thinking Skills & Eye Q by Oliver Caviglioli, Ian Harris and Bill Tindall
Think it–Map it! by Oliver Caviglioli and Ian Harris
Class Talk by Rosemary Sage
Lend Us Your Ears by Rosemary Sage
Exciting ICT in History by Ben Walsh
Exciting ICT in Mathematics by Alison Clark-Jeavons

For more information and ordering details, please consult our website www.networkpress.co.uk

Network Educational Press – much more than publishing...

NEP Conferences – Invigorate your teaching

Each term NEP runs a wide range of conferences on cutting edge issues in teaching and learning at venues around the UK. The emphasis is always highly practical. Regular presenters include some of our top-selling authors such as Sue Palmer, Barry Teare and Steve Bowkett. Dates and venues for our current programme of conferences can be found on our website www.networkpress.co.uk.

NEP online Learning Style Analysis – Find out how your students prefer to learn

Discovering what makes your students tick is the key to personalizing learning. NEP's Learning Style Analysis is a 50-question online evaluation that can give an immediate and thorough learning profile for every student in your class. It reveals how, when and where they learn best, whether they are right brain or left brain dominant, analytic or holistic, whether they are strongly auditory, visual, kinaesthetic or tactile ... and a great deal more. And for teachers who'd like to take the next step, LSA enables you to create a whole-class profile for precision lesson planning.

Developed by The Creative Learning Company in New Zealand and based on the work of Learning Styles expert Barbara Prashnig, this powerful tool allows you to analyse your own and your students' learning preferences in a more detailed way than any other product we have ever seen. To find out more about Learning Style Analysis or to order profiles visit www.networkpress.co.uk/lsa.

NEP's Critical Skills Programme – Teach your students skills for lifelong learning

The Critical Skills Programme puts pupils at the heart of learning, by providing the skills required to be successful in school and life. Classrooms are developed into effective learning environments, where pupils work collaboratively and feel safe enough to take 'learning risks'. Pupils have more ownership of their learning across the whole curriculum and are encouraged to develop not only subject knowledge but the fundamental skills of:

- problem solving
- creative thinking
- decision making
- communication
- management
- organization
- leadership
- self-direction
- quality working
- collaboration
- enterprise
- community involvement

"The Critical Skills Programme... energizes students to think in an enterprising way. CSP gets students to think for themselves, solve problems in teams, think outside the box, to work in a structured manner. CSP is the ideal way to forge an enterprising student culture."

Rick Lee, Deputy Director, Barrow Community Learning Partnership

To find out more about CSP training visit the Critical Skills Programme website at www.criticalskills.co.uk